Using Your Emotional Intelligence to
Develop Others

## Previous Publications

Dr. Linda Gravett: *HRM Ethics: Perspectives for a New Millennium*, 2002.

# Using Your Emotional Intelligence to Develop Others

Sheri Caldwell
and
Linda Gravett

First published in 2009 by
PALGRAVE MACMILLAN®
in the United States—a division of St. Martin's Press LLC,
175 Fifth Avenue, New York, NY 10010.

Where this book is distributed in the UK, Europe and the rest of the world,
this is by Palgrave Macmillan, a division of Macmillan Publishers Limited,
registered in England, company number 785998, of Houndmills,
Basingstoke, Hampshire RG21 6XS.

Palgrave Macmillan is the global academic imprint of the above companies
and has companies and representatives throughout the world.

Palgrave® and Macmillan® are registered trademarks in the United States,
the United Kingdom, Europe and other countries.

ISBN: 978–0–230–61458–1

Library of Congress Cataloging-in-Publication Data

Caldwell, Sheri.
    Using your emotional intelligence to develop others / Sheri Caldwell,
Linda Gravett.
        p. cm.
    Includes bibliographical references and index.
    ISBN 978–0–230–61458–1
    1. Management—Psychological aspects. 2. Leadership—Psychological
aspects. 3. Emotional Intelligence. 4. Customer services—Psychological
aspects. I. Gravett, Linda. II. Title.

HF5548.8.C15 2009
658.4'07124—dc22                                          2009004869

A catalogue record of the book is available from the British Library.

Design by Newgen Imaging Systems (P) Ltd., Chennai, India.

First edition: November 2009

10 9 8 7 6 5 4 3 2 1

Printed in the United States of America.

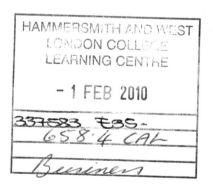

*In loving memory of Wm. Dewey Caldwell.*

*We also dedicate this book to our families, who have supported our writing efforts and promised to read the end product, word for word.*

# CONTENTS

# Contents

# FIGURES AND TABLES

## Figures

## Tables

# FOREWORD

SCOTT WARRICK, JD, MLHR, SPHR

As I settled into my flight from Columbus, Ohio to Los Angeles, I opened "The Emotionally Intelligent Trainer" for the first time. I figured I would get a few pages read, then take a nap somewhere over Missouri. However, as I read further and further into the book, I began to see the widespread applicability of what I had in front of me. I skipped my nap.

People spend years studying the technical aspects of their professions. They invest tens of thousands of dollars in learning their various crafts, whether they strive to become accountants, lawyers, or engineers. However, rarely do they ever consider the practical aspects of how they might one day destroy their own careers in spite of their "sums cum laude" status. This career suicide will not be because they were not technically competent. Instead, they will fail simply because they have not "matured" or "evolved" to the point they are able to control their emotions or egos. In short, you could be the most brilliant professional in the world or have the best company anyone has ever seen, but if you go around "ticking" everyone off, you will become an utter failure.

This book shows the phenomenal difference between the performance levels of emotionally mature people and those who are not. This book uses example after example to illustrate how the highest performing people and the best performing companies do not necessarily have the smartest or most brilliant people working for them. Instead, time after time, those people who build relationships are the ones who come out on top. It is not even close.

To me, the common sense of this concept goes to the core of who we are and why some succeed while others do not. "Ego" is a good thing, but not if you cannot control it. Likewise, your "emotions" can also be a great asset, but not if you cannot control them. It reminds me more of whether or not a car is a good thing. Of course, the answer is "yes." Our entire society revolves around the automobile. However, just as with emotions and ego, the automobile becomes a destructive force to its owner if it cannot be controlled.

This book gets to the basics of why so many marriages in this country fail. One person becomes offended, usually due to a bruised ego, which unleashes a storm of primal uncontrolled violent emotions. The next thing you know, one person has a fork sticking out of his head while the other exclaims, "He made me do it." The assaulting spouse then rationalizes away this attempt at murdering the "better half" by claiming that he "had it coming" in several different ways.

I also see coworkers viciously attacking each other for a variety of reasons, all of which are related to uncontrolled ego or emotions. Coworkers will yell and scream at each other in the most inhumane manner, then justify this primal response by saying something like, "You have to understand, I feel very strongly about this topic." (Sure, now I understand why you act like a witch, give or take a consonant.)

Uncontrolled ego and emotions explain why employees sabotage their employer. Any rational person knows that if they destroy their employer's product, both the employee and the employer will lose. It is an illogical thing to do. However, emotions take over and employees will actually cut off their own nose just to get some blood on the employer they despise. Irrational? Yes, but it happens all the time.

Uncontrolled ego and emotion explains the following.

- We got the Enron scandal, WorldCom, Adelphia, Tyco, and, of course, Martha.
- It is why executives, sometimes the chief executive, think they can have sex in the White House.
- Why Napoleon thought he could take Russia and why Robert E. Lee thought he could march the cream of his army into the union guns at Gettysburg and be successful.
- American auto is dying.

You would expect such behavior to come from little school children, not from the leaders of our age. Unfortunately, this is exactly what your grandma meant when she warned you not to get "too big for your britches."

Sometimes it is the simplest of lessons that evade us most of all.

# PREFACE

We were talking over lunch about the seminar that Linda had just completed for Sheri's organization. The conversation turned to how much fun it would be to capture some of the lessons learned about this training event for the thousands of people every day who enter into the field of training or, as leaders, are charged with educating others. We both have been leaders in the Human Resources field for over fifteen years as well as adjunct faculty for our local universities. We understand that effective training takes planning and careful execution.

The stories, research, and tools in this book are tailored to meet the needs of those thousands of people who feel the weight of the responsibility for education and training in either their vocation or volunteer assignments. We have set about the task of capturing some of the best practices of others as well as sharing our own stories of what went well—and what didn't go quite so well. We want you to learn from our successes and our mistakes, as well as from the ideas of the best and brightest leaders and trainers in the country.

Our central message is that EQ is just as important as one's IQ as a foundation for success in education and training endeavors. We believe that it's important to develop dimensions of EQ such as interpersonal skills and adaptability in order to be successful over the long term, and we provide you with concrete action steps you can begin today toward that objective.

# ACKNOWLEDGMENTS

We'd like to thank the trainers and educators who took the time to complete our best practices survey used as a foundation for this book.

# CHAPTER ONE

## *Introduction*

Last night, Melanie Jones had another late night at the Call Center. Early in the evening, she overhead one of her direct reports (a Customer Service Rep) shouting at one of the company's best customers, Nuts Galore. The rep was not even coming close to being cooperative and could not understand the customer's needs, let alone solve the customer's problem. After overhearing the conversation, Melanie recalled a recent class she had taken on the subject of Emotional Intelligence (EI). She had spent the past several weeks trying to understand why her department was not improving, and Melanie wondered if her staff really had the EI to understand how to listen to and understand their customers' concerns.

The following morning, Melanie came in early and got all her supervisors together. She asked for each of them to share their best customer service experience along with their worst customer service experiences. The "worst" experiences came quite easily from the team. It took a little longer for the "best" examples to come to mind, but with time, they ended with quite a list. Melanie explained to the supervisors that people expect good customer service, so recalling good examples was a bit more difficult. Melanie then shared what she overheard the previous night. This analogy "hit home" with her supervisors. Once Melanie was able to convey tangible examples to her supervisors, she was able to make them understand that it was up to them, as a team, to solve the problems and to help the entire customer service staff to improve.

After brainstorming as a team, each supervisor offered to "interview" a random sample of Customer Service Reps (CSR) and customers. The input from the CSR's and customers was recorded, and the Training Manager put the feedback into a presentation. The feedback was collected from a wide range of experiences, from happy customers to furious customers.

Melanie invited top management as well as the Customer Service Reps and a focus group of volunteer customers to come to a special meeting at the end of the week. The customers voiced their experiences, both positive and negative, as well as their expectations. Ideas and examples of good customer service were discussed; ideas such as—if an order can't be fulfilled, instead of guessing about a replacement, the customer service rep should place a call to ask the customer for substitution ideas.

For the first time the customer service reps (CSRs) were able to directly interact with managers and customers, asking them questions and getting a perspective from them on what made a successful interaction. At the end of the meeting, the customers and reps received a special container of nuts for their participation.

The reps were not only surprised but also impressed that top management and their customers would put so much effort into helping them understand their concerns. It made the reps feel good to know how their efforts fit into the big picture. They could see how important the products were and how much care Nuts Galore emphasized and put into serving their customer's needs. It made them want to be more careful and find ways to help their employer succeed. The following year, Nuts Galore was voted one of the Top 100 Companies to Work For.

While the above case may seem simplistic, such an example helps build a case for how a manager with leadership insight and EI contributes to the bottom line in any organizational setting. Based on data from a variety of sources, we've found that emotional competencies can be a valuable tool for HR practitioners, Trainers, Educators, Managers, and Leaders who need to make improvements and to create standards in their own organizations.

Thousands of studies have found that successful, influential leaders use more EI competencies daily than the average leader (Goleman 1998). EI is most often defined as our ability to understand and express ourselves, understand and relate with others, and cope with life's daily demands.

In the opening example, Melanie used her awareness of her own worried feelings, willingness to be flexible to stimulate a different way of thinking about the situation, and her EI to address the situation, instead of ignoring it, hoping it would get better or go away. EI also includes social awareness, which Melanie used in realizing that the reps at Nuts Galore probably did not understand their customers' challenges and concerns. By holding the meeting and having the focus group session, she helped them to understand the company better.

## Here are some additional practical examples of emotional intelligence in the workplace

### *Selection*

The US Air Force used EI indicators as one criterion to select recruiters (the Air Force's frontline HR personnel) and found that the most successful recruiters scored significantly higher in the EI competencies of Assertiveness, Empathy, Happiness, and Emotional Self-Awareness. The Air Force also found that by using EI to select recruiters, they increased their ability to predict successful recruiters by nearly threefold. The immediate gain was a saving of $3 million annually. These gains resulted in the Government Accounting Office submitting a report to Congress, which led to a request that the Secretary of Defense order all branches of the armed forces to adopt this procedure in recruitment and selection.

At L'Oreal, sales agents selected on the basis of certain emotional competencies significantly outsold salespeople selected using the company's old selection procedure. On an annual basis, salespeople selected on the basis of emotional competence sold over $91,000 more than other salespeople did, achieving net revenue increase of greater than $2.5 million. Salespeople selected on the basis of emotional competence also had over 60 percent lower turnover during the first year than those selected in the typical way without considering EI.

### Productivity

Competency research in over 200 companies and organizations worldwide suggests that in jobs of medium complexity (sales clerks, mechanics) a top performer is 12 times more productive than those at the bottom and 85 percent more productive than an average performer. In the most complex jobs (insurance salespeople, account managers), a top performer is 127 percent more productive than an average performer. About one-third of this difference is due to technical skill and cognitive ability while two-thirds is due to emotional competence. However, this difference increases as the level of the position gets higher. For example, in top leadership positions, over four-fifths of the difference is due to emotional competence.

### Profitability

Experienced partners in a multinational consulting firm were assessed on EI competencies and additional competencies important to the company. Partners who scored above the median on nine or more of the twenty assessed competencies delivered over $1 million more profit from their accounts than did other partners—almost a 140 percent incremental gain.

### Sales

In a national insurance company, insurance sales agents who were weak in emotional competencies such as self-confidence, initiative, and empathy sold policies with an average premium of $54,000. Those who were very strong in at least five of eight key emotional competencies sold policies worth over double than those who were weak in emotional competencies.

Optimism is another emotional competence that leads to increased productivity. New sales representatives at Met Life who scored high on a test of "learned optimism" sold 37 percent more life insurance in their first two years than pessimists.

*Success*

Six emotional competencies distinguished star executives from the average executives when more than 300 top-level executives from fifteen global companies were analyzed. These emotional competencies included: Influence, Team Leadership, Organizational Awareness, Self-confidence, Achievement, Drive, and Leadership.

For 515 senior executives analyzed by the search firm Egon Zehnder International, those who were primarily strong in EI were more likely to succeed than those who were strongest in either relevant previous experience or IQ. In other words, EI was a better predictor of success than either relevant previous experience or high IQ. More specifically, the executive was high in EI in 74 percent of the successes and only in 24 percent of the failures. The study included executives in Latin America, Germany, and Japan, and the results were almost identical in all three cultures.

In the retail field, another emotional competence, the ability to handle stress, was linked to success as a store manager in a retail chain. Success was based on net profits, sales per square foot, sales per employee, and per dollar inventory investment. The most successful store managers were those best able to handle stress.

Research by the Center for Creative Leadership (CCL) has found that the primary causes of derailment in executives involve deficits in emotional competence. The three primary ones are difficulty in handling change, not being able to work well in a team, and poor interpersonal relations. Our research, which we'll share, tracks with CCL's findings.

To put all this into perspective, let's take a real life example of a "star" performer to reveal how several emotional competencies (noted in parentheses) were critical in the success of a computer professional, Michael Iem, who worked at Tandem Computers. Shortly after joining the company as a junior staff analyst, he became aware of the market trend away from mainframe computers to networks that linked workstations and personal computers (Service Orientation). Iem realized that unless Tandem responded to the trend, its products would become obsolete (Initiative and Innovation). He had to convince Tandem's managers that their old emphasis on mainframes was no longer appropriate (Influence) and then develop a system using new technology (Leadership, Change Catalyst). He spent four years showing off his new system to customers and company sales personnel before the new network applications were fully accepted (Self-confidence, Self-Control, Achievement Drive) (from Richman, L. S., "How to get ahead in America," Fortune, May 16, 1994, 46–54, 18).

One final case study comes from the dissertation of Todd Drew of the University of Nebraska (EI Insider Report for February 2008, Todd Drew, 2007). Todd explored the role of EI in predicting the performance of student teachers in his study. Todd utilized the performance reports from college supervisors and cooperative teachers, the student teachers' Emotional Quotient Inventory (EQ-i) scores, and interviews with the student teachers for his research. Todd's study found a high correlation (.61 to .70) between Interpersonal Skills and teacher success.

These examples further exemplify how applying principles from this book can truly impact the bottom line. Since the publication of a best-seller by the same name in 1995 (Goleman), EI has become a major topic of interest in a myriad of settings.

One of the ideas that quickly emerged from the excitement surrounding Goleman's book was the notion that EI was associated with success in various educational and work contexts. A plethora of "new" intervention programs quickly appeared for developing or improving various EI-related abilities. One of the problems with the early literature on EI was the often vague definitions for the concept. EI was consistently treated as a multidimensional construct, but it was often unclear in the early literature what dimensions should be included and what dimensions actually predicted success in different aspects of life. Equally problematic in the early literature was the fact that there was a lack of quick and easy to use, but also reliable and valid, measurement tools for the various EI models that were being proposed (Zeidner, Matthews, and Roberts, 2001).

## So what is EI?

In an effort to help clarify this question, there are currently three major conceptual models: (a) the Salovey-Mayer model (Mayer and Salovey, 1989/90, 1997) who originally defined the construct of EI as the ability to perceive, understand, manage, monitor, and use one's own feelings and emotions to facilitate thinking, measured by an ability-based measure, in addition to the ability to monitor the feelings and emotions of others, and to use this information to guide future thinking and action; (b) the Goleman model (1998), which views this construct as a wide array of competencies and skills that drive managerial performance, measured by multi-rater assessment; and (c) Bar-On (1997, 2000) developed a model that consists of a cross-section of several related dimensions that impact intelligent behavior, measured by self-report within a potentially expandable multimodal approach including interview and multi-rater assessment (Bar-On and Handley, 2003a, 2003b).

Bar-On's model of cross-sections of related dimensions include: intrapersonal abilities (comprised of several interrelated skills such as recognizing and understanding one's feelings), interpersonal abilities (comprised of several related skills such as reading the emotions or nonverbal communication of others), adaptability (consisting of abilities such as being able to adjust one's emotions and behaviors to changing situations and conditions), and stress management abilities (consisting of skills such as resisting or delaying an impulse).

There is growing empirical evidence that the type of competencies most closely linked with EI are strongly linked with an individual's ability to cope with environmental demands and uncertainties. Thus, EI has come to be viewed as an important factor in the quality of one's general emotional well-being, as well as an important predictor of one's ability to succeed both in the classroom and on the job. Regardless of the EI model, most theorists assume that the relevant emotional and social competencies or abilities are quite malleable; that is, it is assumed that emotional and social competencies can be developed and enhanced via appropriate interventions (Bar-On and Parker, 2000b).

The more influential recent work has focused on four key EI dimensions (Bar-On and Parker, 2000b). The first dimension is the ability to perceive, appraise, and express emotion. Emotional perception may involve paying attention to various nonverbal cues (such as facial expressions, tone of voice, posture) in oneself and others. Research has consistently found that the ability to understand emotional behavior in oneself is linked with one's ability to understand it in others. For example, in some settings, a participant, or coworker may not feel comfortable asking questions. Recognizing this, instead of asking if anyone has any questions, ask "What questions do you have?" This simple rephrasing indicates you want and expect questions, so people feel better in asking a question, in general.

The second dimension is the ability to use emotions to facilitate thinking and behavior. This dimension focuses on how emotions influence our cognitive system. This ability can be very beneficial, such as when we use intuition or our "gut-feelings" to help make decisions or be creative. An example from the world of sports might be of the New England Patriots' Coach, Bill Belichick. The Patriots acquired the Miami Dolphin's Wide Receiver, Wes Welker, who was just an average player in his previous three years with the Dolphins and available to all thirty-two National Football League (NFL) teams; however, Coach Belichick took a chance on this yet-to-be-drafted wide receiver, and he became the league's leading receiver in 2007. Why the incredible turnaround? Coach Belichick saw potential. While his previous season's statistics were far from impressive, Coach Belichick went with his gut feeling. He felt that with some practice, Wes Welker could shine. Coach Belichick used his emotions on the field to influence his thinking and behavior off the field. Many managers can probably relate to this. The same thing happens in business where an employee isn't doing so well in one department, but another manager sees potential and gives the employee a try. We've heard the phrase "Don't move a problem" from business leaders before, but sometimes it pays to look beyond the current situation and to dig deeper in order to give people a chance.

The third dimension is the ability to understand and utilize emotional knowledge. As noted by Mayer, Salovey, and Caruso (2002), an understanding about what has led to the experience of a particular emotion is a critical component of EI: "knowledge of how emotions combine and change over time is important in one's dealings with other people and in enhancing one's self-understanding" (19). Think about how often you

children (1935). David Wechsler subsequently included two subscales ("Comprehension" and "Picture Arrangement") in his well-known test of cognitive intelligence in 1939. This test appears to have been designed to measure aspects of social intelligence. The following year, Wechsler described the influence of *non-intellective factors* on intelligent behavior. Again, this was another reference to social intelligence (1940). Following this early description, he argued that the models of intelligence would not be complete until the factors could be adequately described (1943).

Social intelligence came to be positioned as a part of general intelligence, ultimately influencing the way EI was later conceptualized. Scholars began to shift their attention away from describing and assessing social intelligence and toward understanding the purpose of interpersonal behavior and the role it plays in effective adaptability (Zirkel, 2000). This line of research helped define human effectiveness from the social perspective as well as strengthened one very important aspect of Wechsler's definition of general intelligence: "The capacity of the individual to act purposefully."

Contemporary theorists such as Peter Salovey and John Mayer originally viewed EI as part of social intelligence (1990, 189), which suggests that both concepts are related and may, in all likelihood, represent interrelated components of the same construct.

At about the same time that researchers began exploring various ways to describe, define, and assess social intelligence, scientific inquiry in this area began to center around *alexithymia*, which is the essence of emotional-social intelligence in that it focuses on the ability (or rather inability) to recognize, understand, and describe emotions. This book seeks to raise important questions and issues for this field. The questions we address include: What is EI? How is it different from other established constructs within psychology? Is it possible to develop EI? Is EI a better predictor of work performance than traditional measures of intelligence—or, more precisely, which kinds of work performance does EI predict most strongly? Should EI be measured at all? Finally, what is the relationship between ethics and EI?

## Book Layout and Approach

As coauthors, we have elected to take a balanced approach toward writing this book that capitalizes on each of our expertise and experience as practitioners and academics. To this end, chapter 1 has provided an overview of how trainers and teachers, as well as leaders and managers, can use and benefit from the remainder of this book.

In chapter 2, we have laid the groundwork for the book by describing the concept of EI and discussing why trainers and educators, as well as leaders and managers, should develop their EI to become more effective in their roles.

After we make a case for developing EI, we will focus, in chapter 3, on using one's competencies in the needs analysis phase of a training event or any business-related initiative. We will review the four phases of the needs assessment process and provide tools for the emotionally intelligent trainer/leader for each phase. Beginning with this chapter, we will provide at least one training tip from expert trainers in each chapter, which are applicable in varied settings.

In chapter 4, we describe ways in which EI impacts training design. We will share information about tools such as the Myers-Briggs Type Indicator and the Emotional Competence Inventory and discuss how information received from these tools can help assist with the design process.

Chapter 5 will focus on the actual training experience, or "show time." In this chapter we explore how EI can affect establishing a positive and healthy learning environment and the level and richness of participant interaction.

From our experience, we have discovered that many organizations neglect the measurement phase of training, so in chapter 6 we discuss how the emotionally intelligent trainer/leader uses measurement to understand whether meaningful learning has occurred. We will share some excellent tools for assessing the success of training, such as workplace audits and a Return on Investment (ROI) worksheet.

In chapter 7, our focus will turn to how you can develop your training and leadership EQ. We will encourage you to be more reflective about your past training experiences, to learn how to professionally express your feelings in a training environment, to sharpen your skills of observation, and master the art of relationship management.

In chapter 8, we highlight the responses from trainers across the country to a best practices survey we conducted. This chapter will enable you to understand where you fit in the current thinking about training and development and reflect on dimensions of EI that you'd like to enhance to be a more effective trainer or educator, or even a leader or manager.

In chapter 9, we will look to the future and discuss additional applications that require development of one's EI. Critical leadership practices such as succession planning and leadership development will be addressed in relationship to EI.

In chapter 10, we share concrete recommendations for enhancing key dimensions of EI. These suggestions do not take years and years or even months and months to be followed. They are straightforward, everyday activities that anyone can engage in, enjoy, and enhance their EQ score.

In chapter 11, we will summarize key points from the entire book in a checklist format that emphasizes areas that will help you support your organization's strategic business imperatives.

In the spirit of continuing to want to provide practical tools for our readers, in chapter 12 we provide a self-assessment tool that we have developed and tested, which is designed for emotionally intelligent trainers and leaders alike.

Lastly, in chapter 13, our final chapter, we discuss what is next. We expand on some of the suggestions that we have provided in chapter 10 for concrete EQ developmental activities in the form of a development plan. "My EQ Development Plan" is a useable template with additional suggestions about how to complete a development plan in general.

## How to Use This Book—As a Trainer or Organizational Leader

As professionals who either frequently conduct training or offer it to their employees, we are often tempted to let ourselves be pulled into a cycle of "react—develop curriculum—train"—with insufficient time to truly conduct an appropriate needs assessment on the front end or measure results after the training event. If that is a cycle you are falling into, we want you to have the tools and resources you need so as to develop your capacity to engage in more meaningful and productive business and training efforts. Whether it is actually conducting a training session or facilitating a class to conduct a business meeting or lead a business planning session, the tools from this book should be an invaluable resource to you.

As a trainer/leader, you act as a guide and facilitator for the learning experience. If you participate in the process at your highest capacity of EI, you will increase the odds that training efforts will have more impact on individuals and your organization's bottom line. Just as importantly, each training experience will be more challenging, interesting, and invigorating for you. Dare we say it—you may even have fun as a trainer/leader!

Emotionally intelligent trainers and leaders have a heightened sense of self-awareness and empathy for others. They are "tuned in" to the participants in a way that encourages participation, sharing, collaboration, and learning. Emotionally intelligent trainers and leaders provide an atmosphere that invites openness, laughter, and experiential learning. In short, we believe EQ is the basis for an improved experience for the trainer and training participants as well as the leader and his/her colleagues and/or subordinates.

The type of excellent training experience described above doesn't just happen. Trainers and leaders must be aware of the resources and tools that they can rely on to enhance their skill set and natural training and leadership competencies. This book will provide actual scenarios from expert trainers that will leave you with ideas about how to tackle some of your most exasperating workplace and training issues. You'll find these scenarios in chapters 3 through 6. You'll find tools that will help you assess the personality style and learning preferences of workshop participants or fellow coworkers in chapter 4.

When organizations find themselves in a budget crunch, the first area that usually gets the ax is often training. If you can develop training and measure results in a way that emphasizes how training is critical to the bottom line, there's less likelihood that your initiatives will be cut. If this is an issue for you, or has the potential to be an issue in the future, you'll want to read about the ROI process in chapter 6.

Training, like leadership, is an art and a competency that can be developed. We encourage you to use this book to enhance your abilities to plan, design, deliver, and measure the success of your training and workplace efforts!

EI is still a relatively new idea to the organizational world. For better or worse, organizations tend to be political entities. Many organizations trying to promote the idea of EI struggle with the red tape that's often involved in corporate America. As a result, organizations strive to maintain the status quo, or often promotion of the new concept fails due to lack of support from the top.

So why should educators even bother? Being in charge of your own classroom gives you the ideal setting to develop and grow this unconventional concept without the rigidity of many business settings.

In addition, unlike IQ, EI can be developed. While this point may be debated, according to McCrae, "we know a great deal about the origins of personality traits. Traits... are strongly influenced by genes and are extraordinarily persistent in adulthood (Costa and McCrae, 1997)."

Additionally, Bar-On (2000) suggested that, to some extent, EI may be learned and actually improve through maturation and life experience. However, without sustained commitment, effort, and attention, such improvement is unlikely. A wide range of findings from training programs and executive education show evidence for people's ability to improve their social and emotional competence with sustained effort and a systematic program in place.

Perhaps the most persuasive evidence comes from longitudinal studies conducted at the Weatherhead School of Management at Case Western Reserve University (Boyatzis, Cowan, and Kolb, 1995). The students in this study participated in a required course on competence building. This allowed students to assess their EI and cognitive competencies. They were asked to select the specific competencies they would target for development, and then they were required to develop and implement an individualized learning plan to strengthen those competencies. These students were followed through graduation and seven years thereafter to assess whether EI competencies could be developed. The results indicate that EI competencies can be significantly improved and sustained over time.

From a teaching perspective, these results further illustrate the importance of the teacher's role in helping with individualized learning plans and the need to attempt to develop EI competencies as these can be not only improved but also sustained.

When compared to traditional forms of executive education, these effects are much more impressive. Research on traditional MBA programs found just a 2 percent increase in social and emotional competencies as a result of program completion (Boyatzis, Cowan, and Kolb, 1995).

A better understanding of EI can enhance your performance in the workplace. Whether you are leading a training session or a team of coworkers or subordinates, it's important to utilize EI competencies.

## Best Practices Survey

We did not want to rely solely on our own experiences in the workplace or training arena to identify best practices for emotionally intelligent trainers. In order to collect the wisdom of successful organizations and the trainers, educators, and business leaders that have helped them achieve success, we conducted two surveys, the results of which are included in Appendix 1.

The first survey, conducted in the winter of 2004–2005, was designed to capture how profitable, resilient organizations incorporate training efforts into their business plan. We sent the survey to 1,000 public, non-profit, and government organizations in Ohio, Kentucky, Michigan, and Indiana. We received 413 responses that showed some clear trends with regard to the design, delivery, and measurement of training outcomes.

## Some key patterns we observed are

Forty percent of the respondents have a dedicated staff person for employee training.

Sixty-nine percent of the respondents rely on their strategic objectives as a means of needs assessment for training programs.

Seventy percent of the respondents provide Train the Trainer workshops for their training staff prior to placing them in classrooms.

Sixty-five percent of the respondents provide ongoing training opportunities for their training staff.

Ninety percent of the respondents rely on specific criteria such as increased productivity to measure the success of training efforts.

There is a positive correlation across all respondents between having a dedicated person for training and participants rating training as enlightening, fun, and energizing.

There is a positive correlation between using strategic objectives as a needs assessment tool and participants rating training as practical, useful, and informative.

There is a positive correlation between having a succession plan and participants rating training as practical, useful, and informative.

There is a negative correlation between using subject matter expertise as the sole criteria for selecting trainers and participants rating training as energizing, enlightening, and fun.

The second survey, conducted in the summer of 2005, was designed to capture tools and techniques used by trainers in the top fifty successful organizations in our survey. The objective of this survey was to drill down to specific recommendations to enhance trainers' capacity to succeed based on established success criteria. We observed some patterns that were interesting (at least to us!) in this survey as well. Successful trainers and leaders:

1. Include meeting with workshop participants in their preparation phase.

2. Review the organization's strategic objectives to determine how the individual workshop objectives support the organization's mission and vision.
3. Establish specific success criteria for each of the objectives.
4. Demonstrate flexibility with the agenda on training day in order to address the needs of participants.
5. Evaluate training outcomes over the long term in addition to assessing short-term success.

Specific techniques used by successful trainers interviewed for this book will be included throughout the book so that the reader comes away with "news you can use" right away.

# CHAPTER TWO

# The Advantages of Emotionally Intelligent Training

"Something we were withholding made us weak, until we found out that it was ourselves."

—Robert Frost

We believe that Emotional Intelligence (EI) is critical for both personal and professional success. Learning more about EI and in turn applying concepts to your daily life, whether at school, work, or home, will enable you to better motivate yourself and others.

"People who are intellectually the brightest are often not the most successful, either in business or their personal lives" (Mayer and Salovey, 1993). We all have examples of people we know who were good in school but failed in business or vice versa. Sheri's Uncle Joe, for example, barely graduated from high school. He was a "D" student working at McDonald's as much as he could. After high school, he continued working under the Golden Arches, eventually buying a McDonald's of his own. He taught at Hamburger University and now owns several McDonald's restaurants. This is a perfect example that there is more to success than being school smart. Sheri's Mom refers to this as the "College of Hard Knocks," or street smarts. In fact, modern science is proving every day that it is EI, not IQ or raw brainpower alone, that underpins many of the best decisions, the most dynamic and profitable organizations, and the most satisfying and successful lives (Cooper and Sawaf, 1997).

Another example comes from Paul Orfalea, the founder of Kinko's. His unique autobiography, *Copy This*, is filled with life lessons on overcoming obstacles and turning impediments into opportunities. Orfalea is a hyperactive dyslectic, yet despite his learning difficulties he turned the bright idea of making affordable copies for college students into one of America's most successful companies.

It has been shown that IQ may be related to as little as 4 percent of real-world success (Sternberg, 1996). This means that over 90 percent may be related to other forms of intelligence. We believe that the value of EI is priceless. Let's take a look at a couple of specific examples where this is true—in the areas of training and meeting management.

## Advantages of Interpersonal Skills in
## Pretraining Activities

One of the most difficult challenges for leaders and trainers is to figure out how to ensure workshop participants understand the objectives of training and actually apply what is learned, which is why 70 percent of our survey respondents provide pre-workshop activities prior to actual classroom activities. A seminar leader with strong interpersonal skills can observe participants in a casual setting and determine what types of classroom activities will entice people to participate and learn.

If time permits, one popular technique is to hold an off-site retreat to learn more about participants. One of our favorite activities is to ask participants to write down three statements about themselves. Two must be absolute fabrications and one must be the truth. As individuals introduce themselves, they offer the three descriptions of themselves and other participants vote with a show of hands on the statement they believe to be false. At the end of introductions, the person who identified the highest number of false statements gets a prize in acknowledgement of their sleuthing abilities.

Another idea is to meet for coffee or lunch or even a pre-conference dinner. Knowing each other's nuances and quirks, in addition to just their names, allows participants to be less uncomfortable in difficult training day situations. This insight allows trainers to customize the training, and training that is customized is more relevant, more easily transferred, and better retained. Following a dinner the night before a client's management meeting recently, Linda literally threw out 50 percent of the approach she had planned to use to facilitate the next day's meeting. She discovered through listening to conversations around the dinner table that most of the managers were very shy about discussing issues in front of the entire group; however, they were very open in small breakouts of three to four people. Instead of facilitating large discussion groups the next day, she started with smaller groups who then reported out their discussion outcomes.

## Advantages of Emotional Intelligence During Training

One basic advantage during any training session is that when those who are high in interpersonal skills are grouped together they tend to be more cohesive and respond constructively in emotionally uncomfortable situations. Such a positive influence on one another is invaluable to one's department and organization as a whole. Many teams hit "road blocks." We've observed that teams that overcome such setbacks understand their team's unwritten rules about acknowledging emotions. Recognizing what needs to be accomplished will enable the team to manage their collective emotional reactions such as resentment, frustration, or anger, resulting in greater productivity.

This greater productivity is another advantage of trainers and educators that can handle stressful situations with humor and flexibility. Imagine participants in a training session that interrupt or even ignore the trainer. Such behaviors jeopardize the opportunity for successful training—so it's important to acknowledge and appropriately respond to these damaging behaviors.

For example, calling on someone who seems bored will immediately draw that person into a conversation, if for no other reason than fear of seeming "out of it." Or, giving an assignment to a disruptive employee will decrease the number of distractions that person causes, ultimately leading to more productive behavior. It takes EI to recognize the signs of boredom, however, in order to strategize how to energize the person again.

Business leaders can get a variety of ideas from employees. One company president we know who listed safety as a strategic objective got an idea from one of his label clerks. The label clerk's job was to put labels on each product. The backing sheets from the labels would pile on the floor as the labels were removed, creating a safety hazard. She simply asked for a box so the backing sheets could stack into this container, which was an easy and free fix. This thinking "outside the box" enabled the company to maintain their zero accident record. Good for her and good for the boss who listened.

## Advantages After Training

We've observed that people with high EQ scores in areas such as empathy will be much more successful at resolving disagreements that arise following training sessions or meetings. One key dimension of EI is the ability to focus on priorities and adapt to the essential priorities of the moment. We've seen that trainers who tune in to what trainees must deal with in the workplace after the training session and help them prepare for "the real world" during training are the most successful ones. For example, Linda was conducting an educational workshop for a company recently on providing constructive performance feedback. During a break, two of the participants raised a concern: there was a lack of consistency across departments about how to rate employees. That is, "Meeting Expectations" in Quality Control might look different than "Meeting Expectations" in Purchasing. After the break, Linda led a group discussion about concrete ways that the managers in attendance who represented all organizational areas could come to an agreement on the behaviors that constitute each level on the performance evaluation instrument. This thirty-minute discussion led to more consistency in evaluations across the company.

Practicing a new skill daily trains your brain to make it a habit. Current thinking is that it takes twenty-one days to make something a habit, so with focus and daily practice, trainees will be more likely to apply what they've learned. We've observed this phenomenon in one of our client companies. After going through a three-day learning event to learn how to use process improvement team skills such as nominal group technique and force field analysis, one team was able to form and start applying the tools within a few days. Two other teams weren't formed until three weeks later, and by then individuals had to be retrained on how to use most of the tools. The first team, however, was already applying the brainstorming techniques and had incorporated them into other meetings in addition to team meetings. What a difference three weeks can make.

People are born with different strengths in terms of EQ dimensions, although the dimensions, such as empathy, can be learned and developed. Every moment provides an opportunity to enhance EI. It's like "The Wave." It's contagious. One person responds to a situation in a productive way, and another observes and often mirrors the response. Unfortunately, negative behaviors are also contagious. Isn't this where we get "road rage"? The same is true with the upset boss. Yelling at an employee who just made a costly mistake will scare other employees from taking risks, and they may then yell at their employees. Refraining from yelling and working through problems and discussing preventative measures show others how to respond in a similar situation, allowing fellow employees to become better adjusted and in turn become more successful.

That's not to say there won't ever be, or shouldn't ever be, any heated moments during a meeting or training session. There will be! However, we believe that having the courage, the broad shoulders, and the assertiveness to respond appropriately is the key. Whether it's driving away from a potential road rage situation or just talking through a misunderstanding differentiates an emotionally intelligent leader from a "wanna-be."

We believe that in today's fast-paced world there needs to be a balance between high tech and high touch. With on-line communications and voice mails, where facial expressions are not observed, the ability to pick up signals through attentiveness to small details, such as the tone of voice, becomes critical.

Leaders can use these same principles by planning in advance for meetings, performance reviews, or speeches. For example, the President/CEO of Sheri's former employer, Hickory Farms, Inc., had dinner with each department, when he first started to learn more about the employees outside of the workplace. He felt they'd also get a greater appreciation of him and feel less anxious when he called them in for a meeting or asked them to explain their budgets.

When Linda lived in Southeast Asia, she learned the value of a concept called nemawashi. This translates in English to root and circulate, which means that an idea is planted firmly and nurtured so it comes to fruition. There is a concrete application of nemawashi for meeting design and preparation.

A CEO friend of Linda's applies nemawashi when she wants to obtain buy-in for agenda items she plans to discuss at upcoming meetings. Prior to the meeting, she meets with individuals who will be present to chat with them about topics she plans to address and the outcomes she envisions. She asks individuals for their input and discovers where they may differ in their perspectives from her point of view. She listens to what they have to say, and she shares information and background on how she came to the conclusions she has drawn on a subject. With each individual meeting prior to the "big event," the CEO has a clear understanding of her team's viewpoints and has garnered their support for her objectives. She lets individuals know that she expects their input during the upcoming meeting and even puts their name on the agenda by the appropriate topic to indicate that they will lead part of the discussion. There are no surprises, then, on the day of the meeting.

During the meeting, the CEO follows the agenda she has already vetted across meeting participants, although she allows for the introduction of new information and insights to ensure that decisions are made using the most current data. Since there is a clear agenda, though, that has been discussed with individuals prior to the meeting; there is less likelihood that the meeting will be pulled off course. Focus is maintained on the preplanned topics.

The CEO ensures closure at the end of every meeting by making statements such as, "And Jerry you agreed that you'll have this report to Susan no later than 5:00 p.m. on Wednesday, is that right?" This is a tactic that works well to build trust across a team because there's no fuzziness about who is doing what following the meeting. Of course, the CEO is checking in with individuals periodically after meetings to make certain they don't have any questions or there are no barriers to their successfully completing assignments they agreed to take on.

Linda's CEO friend demonstrates the EI competencies of active listening, assertiveness, empathy, and reality testing when she uses this approach to plan and design meetings.

---

*Tools for Developing the Emotionally Intelligent*
*Leader and Trainer*

The EQ Map as presented in the Executive EQ text enables you to chart your relative strengths and vulnerabilities across a wide range of characteristics related to EI (Cooper and Sawaf, 1997). Once you know areas in which you're out of balance, you can take concrete steps to develop a strong EQ.

---

*Training Tip*
An excellent resource for tools for trainers is the American Society for Training and Development's Store (www.astd.org).

For sources that can help you determine which **needs analysis** is appropriate for your situation, go to www.hr-guide.com/data/G510.htm.

For an actual sample of a training **needs analysis** with sample scores and how it works, go to www.businessballs.com/training**needsanalysis**.pdf.

Business leaders are also encouraged to review the survey (in Appendix 1) the authors conducted for practical suggestions that you can use in your own organizations.

*Case Study*

The Widget Team was scheduled to make a presentation to the Executive Management Group (EMG). The team felt this was quite an honor and prepared for two days, ensuring their presentation was perfect. Due to an emergency, the meeting was cancelled. While the Widget Team was disappointed, they anxiously awaited for their meeting to be rescheduled. As time passed and they still hadn't been rescheduled, some of the Widget Team members grew resentful. The Team Captain tried to encourage her team members to remain positive, but she too felt the same way as her team and was afraid she might not get that promotion her boss promised.

*Discussion Questions*

1) What tactic could the Team Captain use to get her team to view the delay in a more positive light?
2) How could the Executive Management Group have handled the situation differently?
3) How can the Team Captain avoid her personal bias of not wanting her promotional opportunity to get in the way of bringing this issue to light?

*Points to Remember*

1) The Team Captain could push aside her personal feelings and encourage her team to use their extra time to conduct a trial run for another department, get their input, and make changes if necessary. She could also explain that this additional time would provide an opportunity to prepare even more thoroughly.
2) Knowing how important this was, the Executive Management Group (EMG) could have selected alternative dates in advance. Additionally, if the entire Executive Team wasn't needed in the emergency situation, perhaps some of the EMG could have kept their appointment and listened to the presentation.
3) Since a substitute date was not offered, the Team Captain could have shown some leadership moxie and asked for an alternative date for the meeting, instead of keeping quiet, not wanting to cause negative attention and perhaps hurt her potential promotion. She could have focused on the fact that the executives were busy with multiple priorities instead of taking the cancellation personally. This would have also brought the issue to the forefront, and she would have gained the respect of her team for being proactive and taking action.

company's overarching strategic plan. For example, Human Resources will want to establish its own Mission (such as "Our Mission is to ensure that the right people are in the right place, with the right skills, at the right time"), Vision, Objectives, and Goals that are responsive to the company's long-term needs. For instance, if succession planning is an initiative that is established by the CEO, senior-level managers may need training in the areas of mentoring, coaching, or providing constructive feedback. The emotionally competent leader is on the case always, whether it's developing a curriculum with the trainer that provides these skills or learning them herself to share with others in the organization.

In Phase 3, each department is assessing internal barriers—or potential barriers—to achieving its strategic objectives. Barriers could range from inadequate technology to low staff morale in a critical area. As department leaders discuss and review these barriers, they should be envisioning what success looks like so they can include trainers in the collaboration process aimed at achieving success. This is an important step that leaders often overlook. As mentioned in Phase 1, include those who know the pulse of the organization. These individuals are usually "in the loop" and are privy to the company's grapevine.

In Phase 4, department leaders assess external barriers, some of which they cannot control. Examples of external barriers are economic conditions, labor skills crisis, government regulations, and competition. Department leaders can work with trainers to address barriers that can be minimized, however. If competitors have a more effective marketing team, perhaps a leading edge training effort can be developed to prepare the marketing staff to outwit the competition.

In Phase 5, the leader or trainer studies the skills gaps that become evident following the company's performance management process. This process can take many forms, but it usually consists of written annual performance evaluations. We're not suggesting that trainers have access to the results of individual evaluations, although that might be a strategy worth trying. We are suggesting that trainers *make an effort to study trends* in skills gaps across the organization. Working closely with the Human Resource Department can help to accomplish this.

Let's say that one of your organization's objectives for its three-year plan is to develop a leadership continuity plan (or succession plan). Discussion questions across the leadership team might be:

- What are the critical positions for which the organization needs bench strength to ensure that the organization grows and thrives?
- What are the core competencies that will ensure success for incumbents in these critical positions?
- Are there specific assignments within the organization that can be provided to candidates for the critical positions in order to build the core competencies?

- Should it be communicated to high potential employees the fact that they are considered high potentials?

From our experience, we've observed that in response to the second question above, dimensions of Emotional Intelligence are always considered part of the core competencies required for organizational effectiveness. Dimensions most prized are interpersonal skills such as empathy and active listening.

An important needs analysis technique used often by our surveyed trainers is supervisor observation. It would be easy enough to simply read over supervisor surveys and select three or four topics they recommend. Our trainers will go one step, at least, beyond this approach. Key questions they consider include:

- Is there a pattern across supervisors in the skills gaps they identify for their direct reports?
- Are there unique needs for a few supervisors in terms of employee skills gaps?
- Is there really a training need with all employees, or are there other issues such as inadequate technology or support from coworkers?

Here's a true situation that happened a few years ago in a manufacturing company. The National Sales Manager came flying into the Training Director's office one afternoon. He was clearly frustrated, and he immediately began to criticize his new administrative assistant's computer skills. He showed the Training Director copies of documents she had created that contained errors and typos. With that, he told the Training Director to send his administrative assistant to remedial classes and walked away.

The Training Director was surprised that the Human Resources Manager would hire an administrative assistant with poor skills for such a high-level person. She had met and interacted with the assistant on more than one occasion, and she seemed very competent and efficient. Indeed, a quick call to the HR Manager revealed that the assistant had done very well on tests given during the hiring process. Something didn't feel right.

The Training Director went to pay a visit to the administrative assistant to see how she was acclimating to her new role. Within minutes, the true problem was evident. The cubicle walls were too low and thin to provide any real soundproofing, and the Sales area was busy and noisy. People waiting to see the National Sales Manager would stop by and lean on one of the cubicle walls, often chatting with the assistant and causing a distraction. If that wasn't bad enough, the receptionist was forwarding all Sales Department calls to the assistant, rather than just those for her boss.

Within one day, the Training Director worked with the administrative assistant and the HR Manager to address the problems discovered. She was provided with a state-of-the-art desktop computer. Her work station was rearranged so she wasn't facing the busy Sales Department, and taller cubicle walls were ordered. The receptionist was reminded to transfer only calls for the assistant and her boss to that phone. Sure enough, the National Sales Manager ran into the Training Director in the hallway a few days later and said, "Thanks for sending my assistant to the training class—she's doing great!" And yes, of course the Training Director let the Sales Manager know what really happened.

We've found that the most effective trainers understand that what people *say* they want and what they *really need* are often at odds. As a trainer we encourage you to take extra steps to dig deeper and discover the difference. A tool that can help you with this process is an Audience Analysis Worksheet, which is included for you in Appendix 2.

Our trainers in the survey also use performance evaluations as a primary needs assessment method. Many indicated that the most effective type of process that supports the needs analysis phase is the multi-rater, or "360 degree feedback," process.

A diagram of a typical multi-rater process ("360 degree feedback") that we use in our client organizations is depicted in figure 3.2 below.

We've observed that competent trainers can use the multi-rater process to discern patterns across departments or divisions. Key questions to explore include:

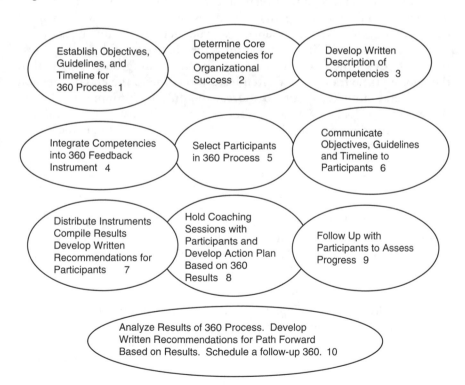

Establish Objectives, Guidelines, and Timeline for 360 Process  1

Determine Core Competencies for Organizational Success  2

Develop Written Description of Competencies  3

Integrate Competencies into 360 Feedback Instrument  4

Select Participants in 360 Process  5

Communicate Objectives, Guidelines and Timeline to Participants  6

Distribute Instruments Compile Results Develop Written Recommendations for Participants  7

Hold Coaching Sessions with Participants and Develop Action Plan Based on 360 Results  8

Follow Up with Participants to Assess Progress  9

Analyze Results of 360 Process. Develop Written Recommendations for Path Forward Based on Results. Schedule a follow-up 360.  10

**Figure 3.2**   "360" Feedback Process

1. Are some divisions or department heads experiencing the same skills gaps year after year?
2. Are employees in certain departments or areas unhappier than others with their supervisor's or coworkers' behaviors?
3. Are there specific areas in which employees are consistently not meeting standards or quality or productivity?

Answers to these questions can guide the design process of training efforts. For example, if the response to Question #2 above is yes, we would consider additional probe methods to determine appropriate training. Methods we've used include focus groups within the troubled divisions, one-on-one meetings with the division head(s), and exploring the competencies required of future leaders in the organization's Succession Plan.

An important needs assessment method that surfaced indirectly in our research is the use of specific success criteria across the organization, such as "zero defects" or "reduction of customer complaints by 5 percent." If meeting these criteria is essential for the company's success, the emotionally competent trainer will include them in the needs assessment and design phase. Were the criteria met? This can be determined in the evaluation phase, which will be discussed in chapter 6. If trainers can consistently understand organizational objectives and criteria for success and design and deliver training that enhances participants' ability to meet those criteria, they will experience fewer budget cuts as time goes by.

One last note we'd like to touch on is the challenge of designing a session that covers the key points set out in the training objectives within the allotted time frame. How often have you come to the end of a session with several more key points to address and only five minutes left before the workshop closes?! We have a tool that may help you, in Appendix 3, a formula for determining the amount of time that should be allotted to each topic based on subject priority.

---

### EI Tools to Live By

The emotionally competent trainer has a toolkit that can be used in all five of the phases outlined in figure 3.1. In this section, we'll describe our favorite tools and those identified by the trainers in our research.

1) Culture Audit (Appendix 4). This survey tool helps leaders determine whether employees across the organization view elements of the organization's culture in a positive light. Elements of culture that are surveyed include training and development, as well as orientation and mentoring.

2) Trust Audit (Appendix 5). This survey tool helps leaders to determine whether theirs is a high trust workplace; that is, whether employees believe in what their supervisors and top leadership say and do.
3) Multi-Rater Feedback Instrument (Appendix 6). Otherwise known as a 360 survey, this instrument provides individuals with feedback from peers, supervisors, and direct reports from internal and external customers.
4) Time Management Self-Assessment (Appendix 7). This tool helps a person gauge how well he or she understands how to set and follow priorities.
5) Quality Dialogue Focus Group Questions (Appendix 8). These guided questions help a facilitator or leader ensure that employees have an opportunity to express their true thoughts on how well the organization is being run or is serving customer needs.

*Training Tip*

You have to go slow to go fast. Crawl before you walk. Take baby steps. In other words, take your time in the needs assessment process so the training design, delivery, and measurement phases will go quickly. Skipping a step to save time may seem like a good idea; however, in practice, this will inevitably lead to a long-term loss.

*Case Study*

The Vice President of Manufacturing has come to you, the Training Director, for assistance with a growing area of concern within his division of 300 employees. He is worried that the 170 manufacturing employees located at your Midwestern headquarters are not accepting the temporary employees being trained for deployment across the United States over the course of the next year. In his words, "Our full-time employees treat the temporary employees like second-class citizens. I'm afraid they're not receiving the on-the-job training they should receive because of prejudice and resentment on the part of headquarters employees." The VP has come to you to ask for a training program to address this growing problem that could adversely affect productivity and therefore profitability.

*Discussion Questions*

1) How can you validate the true problem(s) in this situation?
2) If a training intervention is necessary in your opinion, how will you support the likely cost of ongoing training?
3) Who are the stakeholders in this process and how will you get their buy-in?

*Points to Remember*

1. A culture audit like the one we have provided in Appendix 4 will be a logical starting point to determine where employee issues exist. We recommend that

this instrument be provided to year-round, full time, and temporary employees in order to ascertain how employees feel about the onboarding, training, and development processes. The results of this audit can be used by the trainer to identify pockets of miscommunication and conflict across the organization, including manufacturing.

After the culture audit is conducted, focus groups may be an excellent follow up to hone in on specific problem areas. For example, if Hispanic trainees state that they aren't getting their questions answered or need translation occasionally on instructions, a focus group with Hispanic representatives should be conducted. The Training Director does not necessarily have to facilitate the focus group; he or she can ask for the facilitator to share results. The Occupational Safety and Health Administration (OSHA) rules recommend that training be conducted in the native language of the trainees, so it would be wise to uncover native languages and maybe even allow employees to translate for the trainer if a translator is not accessible.

2. The Training Director should always be aware of the business needs and implications of training activities. The VP of Manufacturing has voiced the concern that trainees aren't receiving the level of training necessary to make a quality product. The business need, therefore, should be surfaced with the input of the organization's cost accounting staff. The following questions are necessary:

- What is the current cost of rejects in plants where newly trained employees have been sent?
- How much supervisor time is required to retrain, and what is the cost of that time?

These types of costs are likely to be much higher than the cost of a culture audit, focus groups, and diversity training.

3. Stakeholders are the new employees, current employees in the headquarters plant, first-line supervisors of new and tenured employees, the VP of Manufacturing, Human Resources, the Receptionist, the Comptroller, the CEO, and shareholders. Actually, everyone is a stakeholder and has potentially different "hot buttons" that need to be discovered and addressed.

We recommend that the trainers do a little talking and a lot of listening to determine the most appropriate approach toward each stakeholder. For example, trainees may fear retribution from coworkers if they participate in a culture audit that asks questions about how well they're received at headquarters. The trainer and senior Human Resources may want to bring trainees together as a group and advise them that they will be asked to complete a confidential survey. Survey Monkey is a great tool for easy, affordable, and anonymous surveys. The process should be explained thoroughly to them, with the help of a translator, if necessary, for Hispanic trainees so that they understand how their anonymity will be preserved. Another approach will be required to appeal to tenured employees. Many companies have a "start meeting" at the beginning of each shift. The Limited Stores is one such company. They share with each employee what is going on for that day in regard to topics such as sales and goals. For this example, a frank discussion at the beginning of shifts to discuss the company's competition, labor force skills shortage, and requirements for expanding the workforce may be helpful. A cost-benefit analysis of the cost of the problem versus the cost of ongoing training will be persuasive for shareholders and company leaders. For new hires, a 30–60–90 day follow-up questionnaire is a good idea.

Quint Studer's book, *Hardwiring Excellence: Purpose, Worthwhile Work, Making a Difference*, offers straightforward, probing questions to ask during this critical initial time frame. These include:

1. Have we lived up to our promise to you?
2. What do you think we're good at?
3. Do you have any ideas that could make us better?
4. Have we done anything in the last sixty days to cause you to consider leaving?

Studer is very popular in the healthcare industry, and there are a number of hospitals that use his protocol and these questions during the ninety-day reviews. It's a nice way to get new hires to think and allows them to provide some feedback or any other comments, questions, or concerns before it's too late.

# CHAPTER FOUR

# Emotional Intelligence in Training Design

We need to know where we're going before we can get there.
—Anonymous

## Key Design Elements

Once the course content and objectives have been selected and sequenced appropriately, the methods (lecture, small-group discussion, e-learning, and so on) and materials (articles, videos, PowerPoint slides, and so on) of instruction need to be selected. Individuals vary, and so do their preferred ways of learning. We think it's important for instructors to promote maximum learning by considering both the audience characteristics as well as the environment (class size, room acoustics, and so on). While this may not seem practical in every situation, compromises can be made, and incorporating as many techniques as possible will aid the learners so that their preferred mode of learning will be presented at varying times.

There are four categories of Instructional Methods, each reflecting a primary characteristic of the methods relevant to the situation and to the learner. These include:

1. Instructor-centered
2. Interactive
3. Individual techniques
4. Experiential learning

### Instructor-Centered

The most common instructor-centered method where the teacher conveys information to the audience is the lecture. Communication is directed one-way. It's an efficient and effective way of getting a message across to a large group of people, particularly if the content is of a lower level. The same is true for questioning techniques or even for demonstrations. Unfortunately, we've seen too many instructors use this method exclusively, resulting in bored, restless students who are only waiting for the minutes to tick by.

The major disadvantage to this type of method is that the learners are passive receivers.

A more effective way for trainers and educators is to use the lecture style in moderation to get their message across and/or in combination with another method. For example, a lecture is sometimes a nice way to introduce the history or maybe science behind a topic, which should be followed by a practical component. Call Center trainers will normally explain the computer system, how to handle difficult customers, and even the company's return philosophy, but it doesn't always make sense until the practical component is added. All lecture and no practice would be ineffective.

### Interactive

Audience participation can be an effective enhancement to instructor-centered methods. While there are practical limitations such as class size and time available, small discussion breakouts can be used for larger groups. Group projects and peer teaching are also excellent methods of interactive instruction. Using the same Call Center example from above, the trainer could involve the peers and practice an actual customer call in small groups of three, where one trainee is the CSR, one is the customer, and the third person is an observer. This is much less intimidating as a way of getting audience participation while simultaneously enhancing learning.

### Individual Techniques

Knowing that individuals learn at a variety of paces, in various ways, individualized learning methods allow learners to work directly with prepared materials at their own pace, receiving information as to their progress at regular intervals. Programmed instruction is a good example of this technique. This is where the objectives are broken into small, sequential steps. The learner is presented with some information and answers a question based on the information provided. Then, depending on the answer, the learner "branches" or proceeds to a specific page and is told whether their response was correct or not and what to do next. Online, or e-learning, experiences are an example of branched—or programmed—instruction. We believe it is important for the trainer to undertake background research to determine whether this is appropriate for the curriculum.

Companies are even using this approach for onboarding new associates. Such instructions allow new hires to learn about their new company at their own pace.

Programmed instruction works for lower levels of knowledge and comprehension. Participants tend to like obtaining immediate feedback and being able to work at their own pace. However, there is a considerable amount of structure involved, which can be an advantage or disadvantage, depending on the learner. Discussions with workshop participants prior to curriculum development can determine the most appropriate choice.

One major disadvantage of e-learning is the lack of face-to-face contact, which many instructors and learners prefer. One solution would be to combine face-to-face contact with computerized instruction. For example, perhaps the entire module may be conducted online; however, the class participants could meet on the last day to present their project to their classmates.

## Experiential Learning

When the learner is actually involved with trying out what he or she has learned, a great deal of engagement can occur. Experiential learning is a common technique when learning a sport or even a technical trade. The same is true with medicine (clinicals) and higher education (student teaching) where the learning is facilitated by experiencing. Role-playing and simulations also fall into this category of learning. In fact, this is the most common way people learn.

The instructor isn't always present during the workplace learning experiences. It is more beneficial to take the time to plan ways to gauge the level of true learning with the trainees' supervisors or customers. Evaluation of true learning and behavior changes can be done through the performance appraisal, customer feedback surveys, or one-on-one discussions with peers. The advantage to this ongoing appraisal of experiential learning is that systemic barriers can be surfaced and addressed before trainees become discouraged and lose their resolve to try out new behaviors or knowledge.

A difficulty associated with this format is that the selection of an instructional method can be complex. The materials used need to match the method of instruction. It may seem next to impossible to try to be prepared for every situation discussed; however, we have learned that that the situation will rarely be ideal or perfect in training. There will always be a glitch or two.

The concept of experiential learning is a key one for business leaders to understand. If you're a leader in your organization, involve your employees as you're developing new products and services. With any new software or project, offer the opportunity for hands on experience. This will alleviate the fear of the unknown and also save time in that if they learn in the presence of others, especially a trainer, when they go to perform on their own what they have learned, they will experience less frustration and, ideally, save time. In addition, there will always be a greater buy-in due to the fact that they were involved in the process. We recently witnessed this as a company was outsourcing their payroll function. The Payroll Manager was completely against the project, as she feared losing her job; however, when HR explained to her that she was still needed to input payroll, that her involvement in selecting the new provider was critical, and that she was crucial to the successful implementation of the new payroll provider, she understood that the change was a positive one.

## Defining the Target Audience

It is neither necessary nor productive for learners to attend something they already know (or think they know). As a trainer or educator, it's necessary to get to know potential students to get a handle on what they truly can and cannot accomplish. Linda learned this early in her management career as she embarked on occasional training for her staff. Her first workshop was actually for a colleague's department and the theme was supposed to be time management. Linda's colleague said that he observed that his team didn't finish assignments on time and always seemed to be late for meetings. His conclusion was that they must certainly need time management training, and he believed that receiving this training from a manager other than himself would "sit better." Linda dutifully prepared a two-hour workshop on time management, using the usual subjects such as meeting management needs and handling interruptions. She did not, however, chat with any of her future students before the workshop. Training day came, and during the first ten minutes Linda shared her objectives and agenda. The looks on the participants' faces clearly said, "oh no, not this again." Fortunately, she stopped and asked the class at large, "is this not a helpful topic for you today?" The resounding response was, "no, time management is not the problem—we know how to manage our time!" After some discussion, Linda discovered that the real issue revolved around workload, delegation, and staffing. She used the two hours to brainstorm solutions to these issues to take back to the Department Director, who was very open to hearing how he could improve the productivity of his area.

Those on the receiving end of instruction, who we'll refer to as "learners," must be considered from the beginning of the instructional planning process. Learners' educational backgrounds, age, motivation, previous experience, intellectual characteristics, language ability, as well as emotional characteristics will greatly affect how much and how well learning will occur.

Consideration of these various aspects of the learner is referred to as audience analysis (Brookfield, 1996). Information can be gathered directly from participants by asking various questions, whether in person, online, or in hard copy format. The analysis can be simple or complex, depending on the availability of the learners as well as time. Regardless, the instructor/leader should only analyze relevant characteristics that are also relevant to the specific situation. Results will assist the trainer with various decisions in the instructional design process, such as level of content, sequencing instruction, and in selecting methods and materials.

Planning for and/or adapting to the seemingly endless variety of learner characteristics is one of the most difficult tasks instructors face. Adaptability is a key dimension of Emotional Intelligence (EI)! Being aware that there are a variety of individuals in any one setting, and utilizing emotional competencies by being perceptive and flexible, recognizing when something isn't working and being willing to start over are the best strategies. In other words, have a "Plan B (and Plan C and Plan D)."

## Selecting Appropriate Activities

Usually, adults become involved in a learning situation by choice and have a clear and specific goal related to his/her own needs. Most of these goals are concrete and immediate. For example, s/he wants to learn a new skill such as Excel or PowerPoint. Adults are also often self-directed learners and want activities that relate to them.

Also, older adult learners in a training session will sometimes require more breaks, more lighting, larger print, louder volume, more time to complete a task, and maybe even more comfortable chairs.

The more basic the knowledge level in a content area, the more desirable it is to use methods and materials that provide concrete experience and examples. As the level of knowledge becomes more advanced and sophisticated, more abstract methods and materials can be incorporated into the training.

Participants tend to respond more favorably when they have input into or responsibility for what s/he learns. One way to do this is with the course objectives. Having secured information prior to the session, whether through an advanced survey, preregistration, or on Day One, you can develop the objectives with the specific learners in mind. One simple technique is to utilize a flip chart and label one page "Parking Lot" at the top. This way, you can survey the group at the beginning of a session regarding their expectations, and/or as topics come up during the class you can add them to the parking lot to ensure they are addressed prior to the end of the session.

The learner should be thought of as a contributor to the instructional design. The degree of the contribution will vary, of course, by the degree of maturity or experience of the learner. While not everyone will be ready, willing, and able to develop their own objectives, s/he will appreciate the opportunity to provide input.

## Sequencing Instruction

Instructional analysis is an important step for Emotionally Intelligent trainers. In certain areas, learners cannot master an objective in the absence of the prerequisite knowledge or skills. Sometimes it's difficult for the trainer to recognize this as s/he might be a Subject Matter Expert (SME) and wouldn't be aware of the basic required competencies. For example, during her swimming class, Sheri asked the instructor how she could wean herself from using a nose plug. The instructor said that she didn't know because she hadn't ever used one and grew up breathing with her nose underwater. She couldn't even understand, let alone explain the technique to Sheri. This type of situation becomes frustrating for the instructor as well as for the learner. We can't stress enough how important we feel it is to listen to students and to try to relate to what they need to know, in a way they need to learn the material.

A caveat is that if the process becomes too rigid, the trainer can't be flexible and spontaneous. We actually like to plan ahead, with two or three options for reaching a learning objective, so that we can be "spontaneous" and select a case study or activity that fits the moment. When teaching business leaders on how they can improve their EI, for example, we have several activities we use, depending on the needs of the attendees, the time available, and the applicability.

### Choosing the Right Trainer or Consultant

Rachel was sitting in the front of the training room, which was a spot she typically enjoyed so that she could see and hear everything that was going on. Today, however, she was fervently wishing that she had sat toward the back so she could work on other things while the trainer droned on, and on, and on. As it was, she could only mentally go through her "to do" list and think about her vacation coming up in three months.

Has this ever happened to you? If not, consider yourself fortunate. This is all too typical from board rooms to training rooms every day in organizations across the country. It does not have to be the norm.

The good news is that there are many trainers available internally and externally from among whom you can select the right one for your training efforts. The bad news is that there are many trainers available internally and externally from among whom you can select! Since even the most (initially) enthusiastic workshop participant can have his/her interest squelched by a poor trainer, it makes sense to take some time when you are responsible for selecting trainers, to ensure you have the right person for the job. In this section, we'll offer some suggestions for finding that right person.

In chapter 3, we discussed the importance of establishing objectives for each training event. These objectives can then serve as a discussion tool when you are interviewing potential trainers. We recommend that you require trainers to provide you with a detailed outline of how they would meet these objectives. The outline should contain timelines for each segment, SMART learning objectives, and notations about participant activities and interaction. Also, ask for several recent references to determine others' experience with the trainer.

We suggest you ask for multiple recommendations because the trainer may only provide details of one or two of their biggest fans. However, if you get a half dozen or so references, you can select which ones you want to call. We suggest you call references from your same or a similar industry, in a like-sized company, and/or the same region.

Of course, trainers should ask you questions about workshop participants and their backgrounds in order to prepare their outline, as mentioned earlier in this chapter. We've included a sample outline in Appendix 9. Once you have trainer outlines, you're in a position to discuss their approach in more specific terms.

In fact, when conducting the interview, ask the trainer to deliver a "practice session" as part of the interview process. This will give you firsthand experience of the trainer in action. This is a very common technique when selecting educators as well. Even in sales, we've heard business leaders handing their pen to the candidate asking for the person to sell them the pen.

When you've narrowed your choice to one or two potential trainers, we suggest you take the observation technique one step further and watch them facilitating a presentation similar to the one you're planning. For example, ask to sit in on an upcoming seminar. We've learned that because a person is an on-air radio personality, for example, doesn't mean he is adept at presenting in front of a live audience. When observing potential trainers, here are some features we look for in particular:

1. How does the trainer respond to participant questions? Does s/he listen attentively and then answer each question thoroughly? Will the trainer acknowledge not knowing an answer and make a commitment to follow up with the participant?
2. Does the trainer identify the workshop or presentation objectives? How close does the trainer come to meeting the outlined objectives?
3. Does the trainer move around and interact with workshop participants rather than stand behind a table or podium?
4. How well does the trainer respond to obvious shifts in the group's attention? Is a break called when the participants are clearly in need of one? Are meaningful activities interjected at appropriate times to keep the pace moving?
5. Does the trainer include opportunities for participants to share their opinions and knowledge?
6. How does the trainer respond to challenging situations such as dominant participants or conflict among group members?
7. What is the trainer's personal style? Is s/he warm and engaging? Is s/he approachable? Will this person be a good fit for your culture?

We also recommend that you check an external trainer's references for topics similar to the one for which he or she will be presenting. A trainer can have subject matter expertise and a great approach for time management and not necessarily be able to present on problem solving. You don't want a trainer who is learning with your group, unless it's an internal person that you're grooming for different training topics, and participants understand this in advance.

Once you've selected a trainer, we recommend that you require a full set of presentation materials prior to the training event. We like to have the materials at least two weeks in advance so that any necessary changes can be noted and made before the last minute. There's nothing that will kill participants' energy level faster than for the trainer to demonstrate early on that he is not covering the topics "as advertised." The training coordinator's role is to ensure that this does not happen.

Look over the trainer's presentation approach. Is the room setup appropriate for the planned activities, in terms of size and layout? Do you have, or can you easily obtain, the AV equipment the person needs? We've learned from experience that if the trainer requests a lavaliere microphone, you need to supply one! Projecting to five people in a meeting room may be just fine; however, projecting to a room of fifty people for three hours is a different story.

Lastly, we encourage you to ask questions about the process the trainer employs to gauge success. Is the person interested in long-term results as opposed to simply a "feel good," first-level evaluation? Does s/he have suggestions for measuring the success of the training objectives after three months, six months, and longer? In short, we suggest you look for a trainer who exhibits an understanding of his or her own competencies and the needs and expectations of workshop participants and their customers.

---

### Tools for the Emotionally Intelligent Trainer

There are many EI models and assessment instruments, each with a different approach, that have been widely accepted by the public due to their validity and reliability. Tools such as the 360 degree feedback surveys are good tools for managers to enhance their performance, for example, and even the DISC personality assessment tool is a widely used assessment tool. Survey Monkey, mentioned earlier, can also be an easy and useful survey tool. Go to www.surveymonkey.com for more information. Emergenetics is the result of extensive research involving over 250,000 adults. Based on the latest brain dominance research, this reliable, valid tool offers a profile to help you discover how you think and behave. The Emergenetics Profile is a unique and powerful tool to help advance your business by giving you insight into not only ways people think and behave but also how you prefer to communicate. It is straightforward and easy to understand.

However, for EI, we have chosen to highlight some of the more prominent tools:

- EQ Map
- EQ-i and EQ-360
- ECI 360
- MSCEIT
- MBTI

The MSCEIT will then dig deeper and seek to understand the relationship between words and feelings, how the person is really feeling, and the ability to manage emotions. For example, was this young boy's emotions mentioned above truly authentic or was he faking his frown and tears to get attention? One has to look deeper into the person's eyes to see if the emotions match the facial expressions.

*Sample questions include:*

1) What mood(s) might be helpful to feel when meeting in-laws for the very first time? (Potential responses are tension, surprise, and joy.)
2) Tom felt anxious and became a bit stressed when he thought about all the work he needed to do. When his supervisor brought him an additional project, he felt _____. (Potential responses are overwhelmed, depressed, ashamed, self conscious, and jittery.)

For more detailed information regarding the MSCEIT, go to: www.emotionaliq.org.

Each of the models discussed above has a unique approach to EI. Depending on your goal, at least one of these should be a useful instrument for you. We highly recommend that you gain further information on the specific model(s) by reviewing it in greater detail.

### The Myers-Briggs Type Indicator

The Myers-Briggs Type Indicator (MBTI) was first developed by psychiatrist Katharine Briggs based on Carl Jung's concept of "types," which he developed in the 1930s. A primary premise of this instrument is that the world around us shapes behaviors and that our preferences toward dealing with others may change over time.

The MBTI is not a test; it's a profile of tendencies and preferences and interests. The MBTI is an excellent tool to help individuals understand themselves better and relate to others in a meaningful way. This instrument has been widely used since the 1980s for career counseling, teambuilding, and even marriage counseling.

We envision the MBTI as an excellent tool to help trainers determine the types of techniques and approaches to use during training activities to shore up their personality preferences. For example, if a person is very introverted that doesn't mean s/he cannot be an effective trainer. S/he will, however, need to develop the ability to verbally interact frequently with co-trainers and workshop participants.

There are eight MBTI preferences that indicate the direction a person's energy will focus: [two]ways of perceiving and taking in information; [two]ways of deciding and evaluating information; and [two]ways of interacting with the environment.

*The MBTI is designed to determine preferences along four scales:*
1. Introversion/Extroversion—Extroverts prefer to direct their energy in interaction with people and introverts prefer to direct their energy inwardly, dealing with their thoughts and ideas
2. Intuition/Sensing—Intuitive individuals prefer to gener- ate new possibilities and anticipate what isn't obvious, while Sensing Types prefer to deal with facts, data, and what can be seen or touched
3. Thinking/Feeling—Thinking types prefer to make decisions based on logic and analysis and Feeling types prefer to consider others' personal values and beliefs
4. Judging/Perceiving—Judging types prefer to have a plan and follow the plan, while Perceiving types prefer to be spontane- ous and flexible

*Here are some sample questions from the MBTI Form G:*
Are you usually
  (a) "good mixer," or
  (b) rather quiet and reserved?
If you were a teacher, would you rather teach
  (a) fact courses, or
  (b) courses involving theory?
Do you feel it is a worse fault
  (a) to show too much warmth, or
  (b) not to have enough warmth?

The MBTI can be an invaluable tool for trainers in terms of gath- ering information in advance about workshop participants. If the trainer knows, for example, that 80 percent of the participants are introverted and data driven, s/he will design small-group activities that involve facts, details, and data.

*Training Tip*
Before you design a training session, meet with a few potential participants. Ask them to describe challenges and concerns they experience around the training topic. Ask them to review and comment on the training outline and planned activities.

*Case Study*
As Training Coordinator for a 5,000-employee company, Sally is responsible for selecting trainers for workshops identified by the company's executives as

important. Sally has seldom experienced such frustration as she is feeling right now. The in-house training session on managerial decision making ended only fifteen minutes ago, and already three managers have stopped by her office to complain. Although the trainer she chose for today's workshop came highly recommended by colleagues in her professional association, the results were a disaster. Sally didn't actually observe this person do a presentation. She conducted a phone interview and was impressed by the trainer's enthusiasm and nice speaking voice.

The complaints she's heard so far include:

- The trainer spent half the training time telling irrelevant "war stories," even when people were clearly restless and bored
- The trainer focused on academic theories, not applications specific to their organization
- The trainer had an annoying habit of constantly pacing back and forth

Sally is frustrated because today's workshop was the first in a scheduled six-part series of management training seminars. Although today's trainer isn't going to facilitate the other five workshops, the three managers who stopped by dropped out of the series.

*Discussion Questions*
1) Is the trainer to blame for the poor results from this training event? Why or why not?
2) How could Sally have ensured the workshop would be effective?
3) What can Sally do to salvage the remainder of the scheduled training?

*Points to Remember*
1) The trainer is partially responsible for the workshop's lack of success. She did not assess participants' needs and interests in advance in order to insert relevant scenarios and examples. Her insensitivity to peoples' restlessness and inattention led her to continue a training style that didn't work. She evidently hadn't ever watched a videotape of herself conducting training, or she would've observed the habit of excessive pacing.
   Sally is also partly responsible for the disappointing results. She relied on a colleague's recommendation without personally observing the trainer in a similar setting. She only conducted a phone interview, so she couldn't assess platform skills or professional appearance.
2) Sally could have increased the likelihood of success by meeting with the trainer in person and observing her in a similar training situation. She could have asked about the trainer's approach toward adult education and experiential learning. Lastly, Sally could have explained how previous successful trainers used on-point case studies and group activities to capture and maintain peoples' interest, and even provide some examples.
3) Sally cannot ignore the fact that the initial workshop might not have been well received. She should immediately review all the evaluations to assess whether the expressed complaints were representative of all attendees' views. We recommend that she meet with the managers (in person or by conference call) to acknowledge that she did not have firsthand experience with the trainer and to discuss what they need and expect from the five remaining sessions. Following this discussion, Sally can share objectives with the five remaining trainers and request outlines with a training approach from each. She, or one of her staff, should also observe trainers in advance to be certain their expertise is at the required level.

# CHAPTER FIVE

# It's Show Time: The Emotionally Intelligent Trainer in Action

You've been through an exhaustive needs assessment process. You've thoughtfully designed a seminar to support specific objectives. Now, it's "show time," the make-or-break component of the training process. At this juncture, dimensions of EI such as empathy are critical. The stakes are high.

Let's go back to chapter 1 for a moment and review the concept of emotional intelligence. *EI encompasses:*

- One's ability to understand one's emotions,
- One's ability to recognize, analyze, and understand others' emotions,
- One's ability to appropriately respond to a situation given the environment and the situation.

In this chapter, we will address how an emotionally intelligent trainer ensures a successful training event, starting with establishing a positive environment for learning, and moving on to specific behaviors that will enhance the experience for participants and the trainer. We'll provide a case study to bring home the key concepts of the chapter.

## Establishing a Positive Environment for Learning

We've observed that not only does an emotionally intelligent trainer design a positive training environment, he or she is in tune with workshop participants during the course of training and can adapt from moment to moment to ensure that there's an energy flow throughout the event. In this section, we'll share some techniques from our research and experience that successful trainers use to maximize learning and behavior change.

We believe that the most effective trainers ask a lot of questions during the training event that are designed to heighten participants' awareness of key points and critical lessons.

Questions we like include:

- What did you just learn about yourself?
- How can you use this information tomorrow?
- What do you think about this approach?
- How can you adapt this technique to your work?
- How would you explain this concept to a coworker?

In addition to *asking* a lot of questions, we think it's just as important to *listen* to the responses and tailor your training style to meet participants' needs. You may have to field some difficult questions from time to time, and we have a summary of suggestions for handling tough questions in Appendix 10.

In a recent time management training session, I (Linda) asked, "How can you use this activity log to plan your week in the future?" One person said, "My experience with activity logs hasn't been very good. I don't know if I want to try these again." I needed to ask some more questions before moving on! I inquired about the reasons why the tool didn't work for her previously. She—and others—were able to articulate experiences with poorly executed activity logs. Now we were getting somewhere. This discussion provided me with an opportunity to share concrete ways to avoid the pitfalls that the participants detailed.

We've seen that emotionally intelligent trainers become students of body language. We've found that body language communicates what people are truly feeling, more so than words. For instance, have you heard trainers ask, "Are there any questions?" or "Does anyone want me to review this segment again?" and then barely glance around the room to determine whether anyone is confused or frustrated? Instead, we suggest that you ask, "What questions do you have?" This shows the participants that questions are expected and that it is okay to actually ask.

You may be wondering how well you interpret body language. Here's a brief quiz we've developed around body language of workshop participants (the answers are in Appendix 11).

### Quiz 5.1

*Body Language Quiz*

1. You're talking with a man whose Adam's apple is conspicuously moving up and down. He is likely to be feeling:
   (a) angry
   (b) depressed
   (c) anxious
   (d) cold

2. You're walking to a meeting with a coworker who is swinging her arms widely as she walks. She is likely to be feeling:
   (a) carefree
   (b) energetic
   (c) warm
   (d) stressed

3. A person you're talking with frequently puts his hand to his cheek. This is signaling:
   (a) rejection of your ideas
   (b) he's daydreaming
   (c) he's evaluating your comments
   (d) anxiety

4. As you're talking with a friend, she is sitting with her hands clasped behind her back. This is probably expressing:
   (a) acceptance
   (b) boredom
   (c) relaxation
   (d) anger or frustration

5. You're walking down the hall with a person who has his hands in his pockets and his shoulders hunched. He is likely to be feeling:
   (a) angry
   (b) confident
   (c) dejected
   (d) bored

6. As you're sharing your idea for a new product with your boss, she is tugging on one ear. This means she is feeling:
   (a) indecisive
   (b) superior
   (c) relaxed
   (d) apprehensive

7. You're telling a favorite joke to a coworker and he places the palm of his hand on his chest as he laughs. This gesture is telling you that he is:
   (a) not really amused
   (b) offended
   (c) sincere
   (d) incredulous

8. You're explaining an idea to a coworker and she is rubbing her thumb under her chin. She is likely to be:
   (a) judging you critically
   (b) anxious
   (c) thinking about how to deceive you
   (d) curious

9. One of your male colleagues is listening to your report during a staff meeting, sitting back with one ankle crossed over the other knee. This is signaling:
   (a) sincerity
   (b) frustration
   (c) combativeness
   (d) disinterest

10. If a person's pupils are dilated, this may mean that she is:
    (a) angry
    (b) stressed
    (c) confident
    (d) afraid

Just as you need to read and interpret others' body language, you'll want to be aware of the messages your own body language is sending. I (Linda) distinctly remember the first graduate-level class I taught several years ago. I was nervous about leaving out essential points in the lecture portion of my classes. I had extensive notes, and I placed them on a small table beside me so that I could refer to them often. I was tethered to those notes. My eye contact was good and I invited class participation, but I confined my movement during class to a two-foot radius of the table. I was very surprised to read this comment (often) in the student evaluations at the end of the quarter: "Linda is not approachable. She doesn't walk around and talk with us during class." That was *not* the message I intended to send! Now when I teach, I walk around freely, notes in hand for easy reference. It works for Oprah Winfrey, why not for me?!

We believe it's important to acknowledge that workshop participants have expertise and experience. Yes, the trainer has (or should have) a high level of subject matter expertise. In our research, we found that workshop participants weren't especially enthralled with trainers who had knowledge of the topic but didn't invite participant discussion and interaction. People want to share their own experiences and suggestions. To be successful as a trainer, it's necessary to foster a give-and-take dialogue within the classroom (without letting only one or two participants dominate). Here's an example provided by one of our surveyed trainers:

> I was facilitating an in-house workshop on the business case for diversity initiatives. I noticed that a guy in the back kept making comments to people at his table. The entire class became distracted. So I broke the class into breakout groups to discuss some real-world scenarios. I asked 'the talker' to be the reporter for his group. That quieted him down for the rest of the morning...at least from the sidebars.

Another critical skill is showing respect for participants' feelings. Especially in a technical training session, participants may feel insecure about their ability to learn new skills. The trainer who fosters an environment in which all questions are valid and can be repeated more than once will be valued and appreciated. We know of a computer software trainer who walked into the training session for the first of several classes wearing a giant fake thumb on his left hand. His opening line, as he held up his hand, was "This is probably how most of you feel right now...and that's normal!" Everyone laughed, and tension was eased tremendously. If a workshop participant is feeling anxious, frustrated, or unmoved by an explanation, that feeling should be acknowledged and not discounted. Then the trainer can move forward to address the person's unease, starting with a question such as, "What would help you feel more comfortable about this tool/technique/approach?"

Once a positive workshop environment is established, here are some additional steps you can take to sustain an environment conducive to learning.

### Balancing Listening with Telling

Think about someone you know who you believe to be an excellent listener. What exactly do they do (or not do) that leads you to characterize this person as a good listener? Perhaps some of the descriptors you identified are similar to ours:

- Maintains eye contact
- Asks questions
- Doesn't interrupt when you answer questions
- Doesn't judge or appear shocked by what you're sharing
- Paraphrases to ensure understanding

A critical aspect of interpersonal skills is the ability to listen actively, and the result is that participants want to share their ideas, make suggestions, and ask questions. This in turn promotes an energizing and productive training environment, one in which there's an undercurrent of curiosity and excitement.

On the flip side, consider how you would respond in this situation:

Mary tuned out two hours ago, but unfortunately the training is scheduled for three more hours. Three...more...long hours with Joe, the trainer. Joe has been expounding on his sales exploits without pausing for breath since early morning. At first, his stories were interesting. But no one can get a word in to make a point or ask a question. Yes, he's an experienced sales professional...but Mary wants to learn from others in the workshop. If Joe would just shut up for a minute...

Learning for adults must be interactive and experiential. Students won't experience anything except drowsiness if trainers aren't astute enough to balance "telling" and "listening."

## Encouraging Interaction

If you're a trainer, you've probably experienced a group that was intro-verted and (seemingly) unresponsive to your attempts at promoting a two-way dialogue. We'll share some approaches from successful trainers that will jump-start your sessions when this happens.

Our first message is for you extroverts out there, you know who you are! The message is this: a moment of complete silence is OK. Ask a thought-provoking question. Pause. Let people know they can have time to think. Not to worry—someone will respond. We don't recommend, however, that you goad participants into responding with comments like, "Come on...somebody knows this," or "Don't you guys talk?!"

Consider asking two or three people in advance to be prepared to share their perspective on some of the discussion questions you plan to use. Even introverts will be talkative during class when they've had some time to process their thoughts and ideas. For that matter, why not share your workbook in advance for people to review? If there are articles or books you intend to use as a reference, provide an advance reading list.

Sometimes individuals are not as comfortable discussing questions or concerns in front of the entire group as they are in small breakouts. Do some homework to discover which participants work effectively together. Mixing up groups can also be an excellent way for participants to meet coworkers in other departments and expand their understanding of others' work.

Sometimes genuine interaction is squashed by the presence of supervi-sors in the training room. A direct report isn't as likely to be forthcom-ing with questions or identify problems if her supervisor (or supervisor's supervisor) is in the room. The situation is tricky. On one hand, people want to know their supervisors receive training and learn techniques to develop their skills. On the other, some people don't want supervisors in *their* training session. We believe trainers should explore how participants feel about having joint training sessions before the training is designed, not during training.

You can have it both ways. Bring supervisors and line staff into train-ing sessions together, but plan some breakout sessions where each group spends time with their peers. For example, separate brainstorming sessions could occur as a breakout, with the line and supervisory staff coming together to report out and do some action planning at the end of the day.

Another factor that affects workshop interaction is the diversity of its participants. I (Linda) conducted an in-house seminar recently on the topic of communication between men and women in the workplace. The group that sponsored the workshop was a female executive's forum com-prised of top-level women within the organization. Men and women were invited; however, 70 percent of the participants were women. One of my initial questions that I used to open discussion was, "How do you think men and women differ in the way they give instructions in this company?" Female hands shot up, responses were swift and impassioned. Not one male responded.

My choice was clear: let the male participants sit in the back in their huddle, disengaged from the activities, or find a way to pull them in right away. Fortunately, I had met with some of the participants before the training (men and women alike). The men told me that they felt misunderstood and stereotyped (!) as uncaring and pushy. They worried that regardless of what they said, the female workshop participants would mistrust their true intentions. Knowing this, I used this moment to lighten the tone and encourage participation with a skit that the focus group helped me write. One of the guys in the focus group participated in the skit, about male and female coworkers passing along a directive from the company president. We exaggerated every male and female stereotype imaginable. The skit was funny and people couldn't help themselves; they laughed, and the interlude loosened the men up and they started to participate.

People who have a high level of interpersonal skills express sensitivity to cultural norms. Since our companies today are becoming more diverse in terms of customers and employees alike, it's important to show an interest in learning others' customs and traditions. I (Linda) learned this lesson early in my career when I lived in Japan. As the Accounting Manager for an Air Force base, I managed a staff of nine, eight of whom were Japanese natives. So that I could foster better communication, I pushed myself to learn Japanese.

At the close of my first year managing the department, our office decided to change some of our accounting procedures. I elected to have an off-site workshop and conduct staff training myself, in Japanese. During the workshop, I asked for questions but received none. My staff smiled warmly at me all day long, took some notes, and told me at the end of the day how excellent the training was. On Monday morning, however, when the staff was supposed to put the new procedures in place, it became abundantly clear that my instructions were not completely understood. I was extremely frustrated and went home that evening to have an "over the fence" conversation with my Japanese neighbor.

I shared with my neighbor how I had done most of the training in Japanese and how responsive the staff seemed to be. But, I said, "they just don't get it." My neighbor bowed politely and said, "No, Linda-san, you don't get it. In our culture, a teacher is revered. Students would not cause a teacher to lose face by asking too many questions. It would show that the teacher was not a good teacher." What an "aha moment" for me! I set up another training day and made two adjustments to my training style. First, I shared with my staff at the beginning that I appreciated their cultural norm of not asking questions of the teacher. I asked for their help in working within my American cultural norm of asking a lot of questions. I shared with them that they would make me look good by asking many, many questions! They nodded, they understood. They asked questions. Additionally, I provided mini-quizzes throughout the day so that I could review them during breaks and get a feel for how well people understood each segment. I could then clarify key points that weren't being grasped the first time.

Yes, this adjustment worked. I'm eternally grateful for the valuable lesson I learned from my Japanese neighbor.

## Using Emotions: The Skillful Trainer

Another important aspect of Emotional Intelligence is the capacity to use one's emotions, whether they are anger, joy, empathy, or frustration, in a way that is productive and positive. For example, consider this scenario from a training event:

> Mary was at the end of the training day and "at the end of her rope" in terms of her frustration level. One of the workshop participants, Joe, had just interrupted her explanation of a problem-solving technique. He had been doing this all day long, and it really was getting to her because she was having a difficult time concentrating as it was. Mary was leading a workshop on problem-solving for the first time and was feeling insecure about her level of expertise. Joe, an engineer, was clearly experienced in this area and Mary felt that he was just showing off. As Joe started to interrupt, Mary held up her hand to ward off his question and said curtly, "wait until I'm finished with my explanation." Joe, and everyone else in the room, looked stunned.

Early on in the training day, Mary could have made the decision to include Joe in leading some discussion groups or capturing peoples' comments on a flip chart. This might have alleviated his need to insert himself at inappropriate times and could have provided Mary not only with extra time to think about the concept being put on the flip chart, but also with an ally instead of a foe. Instead, Mary was so caught up in her insecurity about leading this workshop that she had a hard time feeling empathy for a person who himself might have just needed a little extra attention. On the other hand, it's possible to feel too empathetic and get caught up in another person's feelings, to the detriment of the training environment. Let's look at another scenario:

> Jim is feeling depressed and down, and it's only two hours into the training. As the workshop facilitator, he usually is energetic and upbeat. However, Susan, one of the participants, came into the training this morning with tears in her eyes. She shared that her boss had harshly criticized her right before she came to the workshop and she was fearful that she might be fired. Susan works in the same department as Jim, although they have different supervisors. Every time

Jim looks at Susan's face, he gets more and more down and less able to concentrate on what he's doing.

In the above scenario, Jim is letting his empathy for a coworker interfere with his effectiveness as a facilitator. He's not helping Susan and he's not adding to the training environment by acting down and distracted. Feelings like this can be very contagious, and if this keeps up, the energy level of the entire group could be adversely affected.

In *Primal Leadership*, Daniel Goleman suggests, "The best leaders have found effective ways to understand and improve the way they handle their own and other people's emotions" (*Primal Leadership*, Daniel Goleman, page 4). As a trainer, workshop participants look to you to provide a positive learning environment. If you are clearly angry, frustrated, anxious, or moody, the training atmosphere will be compromised. So, how does one get to a mental "place" that's relaxed, positive, and enthusiastic each and every time regardless of their own true feelings?

We have some techniques that we use prior to conducting a training event that help us sustain a level of energy and calmness and in turn manage our emotions regardless of how others are behaving. Activities that help us to gain focus and concentration prior to training is to practice either yoga or T'ai Chi for 15–30 minutes. Both are ancient arts that help one to call in energy, flex tired muscles, and reach a level of calm. During particularly stressful training events, we may find a quiet place and take fifteen minutes during breaks to do a few light exercises or practice deep breathing. If participants want to join in, we invite them along!

Unfortunately, there are some unnerving behaviors that workshop participants can engage in that will dispel one's relaxed frame of mind. In one of my (Linda) first experiences leading a training event, I was faced with an entire class that was angry about the way the organization's supervisors conducted performance evaluations. As a member of the organization myself, I must say I wasn't happy about the process either.

I decided that we could use our anger in a positive way and channel that energy toward developing some recommendations for changing the system. When it became apparent that this topic was distracting and we couldn't move on until it was addressed, I stopped the program and led a "force field analysis." We brainstormed recommendations for an effective performance evaluation process, and I captured participants' ideas on a flip chart. We discussed forces working for and against the recommended process change, along with suggestions to minimize the potential barriers. I noted that these suggestions would be taken to my boss (a vice-president) immediately after the session. The brief venting process helped people calm down, and the suggestions went to a person with the position and power to take action.

There are some types of training when the need for an empathetic trainer is truly critical. We've found that training in the areas of conflict resolution and managing workplace diversity are two such instances.

These topics can bring to the surface imbedded stereotypes and hurt feelings, and the trainer must be able to effectively deal with these emotions. Here's a true story:

> Linda was facilitating a diversity training session in a manufacturing plant. The participants were line employees who had very few opportunities to attend training prior to this workshop and didn't have much in the way of social savvy in a training environment. In order to demonstrate how diverse teams can work effectively by leveraging their diverse perspectives and experiences, Linda had the trainees doing an activity that required them to throw softballs to one another while standing in a large circle. One of the guys in the circle hit the woman he was throwing to in the arm, and the softball bounced into the middle of the circle. He immediately called out, "See...women can't catch." The woman's feelings were clearly hurt, but she picked up the softball and the activity continued to completion.
>
> Linda's dilemma was how to turn this situation into a teachable moment. After checking in with the woman who was hit with the softball to make certain she wasn't hurt, Linda conducted a debrief for the activity. Instead of calling out the dropped ball incident, Linda asked two questions: "How did you use each others' talents and ideas to complete the assigned activity?" and "What did you do to support and motivate each other; what could you have done more effectively to support one another?"
>
> The key was not to shine a spotlight on any individual faux pas and stereotypes but rather to focus on the efforts of the entire team.

## When to Throw Out the Program Agenda

My (Linda) first opportunity as a trainer came when I was working with a Circuit Court of Appeals. I was "loaned" to other areas of the Court from time to time to facilitate first-line supervisory training. The first session I did was for a group of Probation Officers. Their manager requested that I conduct a time management workshop because his team was always complaining about not having enough time to complete priority projects.

I did the up-front preparation we've suggested earlier in this book—I interviewed three or four workshop participants in advance and found out their most thorny time management issues. I prepared a three-hour seminar based on the manager's objectives and the participants' responses to my questions. About thirty minutes into the training, I couldn't help but observe that people seemed restless and disinterested. Instead of forging ahead, I stopped and inquired whether the material was helpful or if I needed to go more in depth on anything covered to that point. Almost everyone looked at their feet immediately, but one kind soul responded by saying, "For this off-site, we don't really need or want time management techniques. We've been there and done that." I had to make a decision: do I plug away with the agenda for two and a half more hours, knowing they'll be bored and the time will be wasted, or do I just dismiss the class and give them a free morning? Or, do I ask whether there are other topics that are more critical that we could address. I chose option three.

Several people raised their hand and suggested another topic and said that their manager neglected to ask them what would be most helpful to cover. They asked if I could share some ideas about practical decision-making techniques. I could. I didn't have a formal program prepared; however, I shared real-world scenarios with decision-making dilemmas and broke them into teams to discuss. Then, I used the flip charts provided to demonstrate techniques such as Force Field Analysis and Affinity Diagramming. The class was very grateful to have covered a topic that was truly a need, and I learned a valuable lesson about digging deeper in the needs assessment process!

Early on in my consulting career, I (Linda) was invited to facilitate a series of workshops for a culinary institute on some of the "soft skills" that restaurant owners and head chefs had to acquire, such as performance management and coaching. The students were barely interested in these types of topics—they wanted to learn how to prepare and serve food. I came to know this while going in and eagerly set about making my sessions interesting and interactive so that students would enjoy the departure from their typical curriculum.

When I entered the culinary institute's conference room where the training would occur, I couldn't help but notice that this area of the building was old and dingy. The tiles on the floor of the conference room were dirty and cracked. The tables that were set up were not all stable and were of various sizes—they were clearly pulled from nooks and crannies all over the school. I had toured the kitchens earlier in the week, and they were spotless and new. I assumed the other spaces in the school were of the same caliber.

Within the first half hour of the workshop, it was crystal clear that the students were not enjoying the material, which was around the topic of leadership skills. As I covered the objectives, more than one person interjected that they wouldn't be able to use these concepts for years to come, if ever. There was a lot of whispering and side conversations as we moved into the lesson plan.

I stopped in the middle of a sentence and said to the class, "I'm willing to throw out the agenda and cover what's really on your minds. What do you need to know as chefs in the restaurants that you're working in now or plan to seek employment in?" They just looked at me. I picked up my class notes and threw them on the floor. They laughed.

One person raised his hand and said, "We'd really like to be leaders here, at the school. We're not happy with the way the school is run and how classes are organized. We're not happy with some of the chefs that are brought in and their approach to teaching." I looked around and asked whether this concern was shared by others. Every person in the class raised a hand.

I introduced the class to the concept of Force Field Analysis, with the discussion topics of "Forces Working for Success as Students" and "Forces Working Against Success as Students." We identified positive factors they could leverage and noted factors that were barriers, then moved on to the brainstorming steps they could proactively take to minimize the barriers. They became empowered with this knowledge to take action. The class left with an action plan and individual assignments for carrying out the action plan—just like the leaders I was trying to teach them to be!

Several of the successful trainers we interviewed said that they will occasionally throw out their preplanned agenda or go "off-course" if the classroom discussion warrants. We recommend that trainers discuss this possible tactic with the Training Coordinator or person bringing them in to conduct the training, so they aren't unhappy when word gets back to them that the agenda they wanted covered wasn't covered in full.

We are not promoting a "loosey goosey" approach toward conducting training, where there's no planned agenda and everything is free flowing. Unless you're in an "open space technology" environment, some structure is necessary to assure that key points are addressed. We're suggesting that trainers remain open to veering off the agenda occasionally to be certain to cover those areas that are most relevant to participants. The more up-front time is spent in the design process, the less likely will this be necessary. By the way, you may not be working alone in the design and delivery process. If this is the case, we've provided a checklist for doing team presentations in Appendix 12.

*Training Tip*
If two workshop participants are engaging in a side conversation, continue talking but walk over to an area a couple of feet away from the two that are having the sidebar. Without your saying a word to them, they'll get the message that their conversation is distracting.

*Case Study*
Bill rushed into the training room ten minutes before the scheduled start time. He had hoped to arrive early enough to test the AV equipment and place handouts on the tables before participants started coming in. He looked around as he walked toward the front of the room, and he could tell that about half of the registrants were already there. Typically, Bill liked to greet people before he began his workshops, but today he'd just have to forego that nicety and make sure he was set up. He is an external consultant coming into the organization's training room, so he's sure that everyone knows where coffee is located and is acquainted with at least one or two coworkers at the workshop.

Bill hurriedly set up his laptop and projector, focusing on what he was doing instead of people coming in and out of the room. At five minutes after scheduled start time, he was ready to go. He mentally shifted into "show time" and looked up and greeted the class with a smile.

Bill was dismayed at what he saw as he looked out over the room. The coffee and continental breakfast that was supposed to be set up in the back of the room wasn't there. There were four tables set up in rounds to seat eight, instead of six tables set up to seat six. All the participants were huddled around two of the tables. Supervisors were supposed to provide participants with their workbook materials the previous day, yet only about half the participants had a workbook in front of them. Bill gulped, but cheerfully welcomed everyone and told his favorite joke that always loosened people up. No one laughed.

Bill ignored the lack of response and went right into his slide presentation, with the first slide showing the workshop objectives. He had been told that these objectives were going to be shared with participants in advance, so he only spent a moment reviewing them before moving on to logistics such as breaks and lunch arrangements. He thought this would settle people in to concentrate on the topic at hand, but he sensed a restlessness across the room.

Bill moved on to a breakout activity with a case study intended to generate an energetic and lively discussion. When he asked people to "count off" for the breakout groups, they seemed reluctant to leave the table where they were sitting. Bill just joked about "shaking things up" as people slowly moved into discussion groups.

There was a tenseness in the air for the first ninety minutes, and by the time he was ready to call the first break, Bill didn't know who was more uncomfortable— him or the workshop participants. This was not going as planned, and he had to come up with something during the fifteen-minute break to turn things around.

*Discussion Questions*
  1. What could Bill have done differently to set a positive tone at the beginning of the workshop?
  2. Do you have any suggestions for how Bill can salvage the day?

*Points to Remember*
  1. There's no question that it's important to be prepared with room setup, AV equipment, and handouts prior to the start of the workshop. If Bill wanted to be ready at the appointed start time, he could have arranged his schedule so that he would arrive at least thirty minutes early. If traffic or some other delay was going to result in his running behind, he could have contacted a predetermined person at the organization to help him put handouts on tables or ensure the room was set up appropriately. Greeting people as they enter a workshop is a way to make them feel welcome. Having coffee or juice for a morning workshop is critical! Even if he had to cut a portion short later in the day, Bill would have provided a more welcoming environment if he made sure that participants were greeted, had coffee, were directed to a table, and had workshop materials in hand.

Bill could have also delayed setting up the AV equipment and greeted participants instead. Then, he could have adjusted his schedule and formed groups at the very beginning, allowing him time to then set up his laptop and projector.

Once Bill started, he had an opportunity to get the "pulse" of the room early on, when people didn't respond to humor that normally was effective. He missed the chance to align objectives by not checking to see if the stated objectives were in tune with participant expectations. He framed the workshop as being structured and rigid by staying on task the moment he walked into the room, head down and "on a mission."

2. Bill has a very short time to decide how to capture peoples' attention and interest. We would take the participants back to the beginning of the workshop and revisit the objectives. Bill should be candid and admit that he was not effective in drawing them in and setting a positive, interactive tone at the beginning. He can ask for their forgiveness and help in "regrouping." If a trainer is sincere, people will generally give him or her a second chance. He could start with the objectives and ask them to add their expectations and issues with the topic, writing them down as people talk. He may need to throw out some of his agenda items and focus on two or three areas that are of most concern to the participants. He may need to lead a discussion of real time case studies rather than use prepared scenarios. Most important, he needs to let people know that he's willing to be flexible in order to cover areas that will be most helpful to them.

C H A P T E R   S I X

# Emotional Intelligence and the Measurement Process

Before we discuss ways to measure training results, we believe it's important to address *why* trainers should evaluate training results. There's no doubt that it's tempting to ask participants to complete a one-page "how'd you like it?" type of evaluation and be done with it. However, we suggest that more in-depth evaluation be conducted for these reasons:

- To ensure that participants' behaviors and skills following the workshop are aligned with the organization's strategic objectives and business imperatives
- To assess what activities during the training event were well received and supported the learning process and what activities were not successful
- To help identify participant skills gaps (or organizational deficiencies in terms of resources)
- High performing employees (at the 84th percentile) have from 40 to 80 percent greater impact on firm performance (*The HR Scorecard*, Becker, Huselid, and Ulrich, 2001, Harvard Business School Press, 90)

A trainer may provide an excellent workshop on time management. When the participants really need and want decision making skills, however, they won't be excited by a time management workshop of any caliber. Targeted training to address the skills and competencies that will help the organization survive and thrive should be the priority, and ongoing evaluation should focus on whether trainees are developing those competencies.

Trying innovative and different activities during training is certainly an approach we recommend. However, the follow on to this approach should be an assessment of how well these new approaches met the participants' needs. Were they fun? Did they promote learning? If not, don't include them in future training sessions!

The role of a trainer is to facilitate learning in the classroom, and they're also attentive to resource needs outside the classroom. We often hear these statements from participants in our training sessions:

"My boss needs to be here. She doesn't use these concepts."

"This is good stuff, but I don't have this program on my computer."

"My supervisor won't give me time to practice using this new material."

These types of statements should provide a clue that follow-up meetings with participants' supervisors and managers are necessary to advise them of the resource their staff will need to ensure that new competencies are developed and nurtured. Participant focus groups and surveys that follow three to six months after training events are excellent techniques to gauge whether sufficient resources have been provided.

## Understanding Transfer of Training Concepts

Every successful trainer we interviewed projected a deep understanding of the transfer of training from the classroom to the workplace. The pattern that we observed across effective trainers is that they understood that training outcomes must have meaningful measures. In this chapter, we'll discuss how trainers with high scores in the EI components of empathy and assertiveness measure training results and how that measurement orientation positively impacts their organizations.

One of the senior managers we've worked with attended a conference on leadership skills. He (rightly) discerned that the competency of active listening was one in which he needed development. Whenever his staff would stop by to talk with him in his office, even if he was on the phone he'd wave them in with, "come on in…I'll be right there." As staff members mentioned their question or concern, the manager would be on the phone, shuffling papers, or otherwise engaging in multitasking. His boss told him to attend the leadership conference and focus on building his listening skills.

During the conference, a couple of his direct reports also in attendance observed that the manager would thoughtfully respond to in-class discussion questions and case studies. They thought, "wow—he finally understands what it takes to be a good listener!" However, back at the office, the manager's behavior was just as inattentive as before the conference. How could he have participated so positively in the training and not transferred what he had learned?

Participants' time, trainers' time, and the organization's money are all wasted when there is no transfer of learning from the training environment to the work setting. Emotionally intelligent trainers design success criteria into each program to gauge what works—and what doesn't work—in facilitating the transfer process.

For a true transfer of training concepts to occur, these factors must be present:

- Trainees want to use what they've learned in the workplace
- Trainees understand how to use what they've learned in the workplace
- Trainees have the resources to use what they've learned in the workplace
- Trainees have the support of coworkers, managers, and customers in using what they've learned

A large part of the trainer's role is to establish a training environment that motivates people to want to use new skills or techniques they learn. We'll discuss measures that indicate whether this is occurring. Trainers also are responsible for teaching the "how," or the application of new learning, and this can be measured. Trainers usually don't have direct influence over participants' resources in the workplace or the level of grassroots support; however, they can take a leadership role and indirectly influence these factors.

Five Levels of Measurement, Reaction, Learning, Behaviors, Results, and ROIA trainer's ability to receive constructive criticism, are clearly tested at the reaction-level of evaluation. The trainer's ability to "read" participant reactions during the course of training and in the closing minutes is critical to understanding whether a meaningful experience has occurred.

A couple of years ago, Linda was asked to observe some in-house training events for a client company. One of the daylong programs was on customer service, using interview and survey tools—at length—to assess customer needs. The trainer asked for expectations during the first half hour and even wrote them down. However, she did not once refer to those expectations and ask if they were being met. She even spent an hour on one topic that participants specifically said they did not have an interest in, and during this hour it was clear to Linda that the class was bored. At one point, she asked for a ten-minute break just so people could escape for a few moments and she could recommend that the trainer move on to one of the topics the class had indicated a strong need to cover.

The participants did fill out a brief evaluation on the course content, pace of the workshop, and the knowledge of the trainer. Linda noticed that the trainer did not even glance at the evaluations. When Linda asked how she thought the workshop went, her response was, "whew...I thought I wasn't going to get through all the material on the agenda, but I did!"

This trainer needed to be brought to the level of conscious incompetence before we could even begin the process of developing her level of empathy as a trainer.

We believe that a reaction-level evaluation, like the sample in Appendix 13, is an important element of the measurement process. However, we've all probably experienced energized, engaging presenters to whom we reacted positively during the presentation. Two days afterward, though, we couldn't recount even two or three key concepts let alone discuss how to apply them in the workplace. We must move on to higher levels of evaluation criteria, beginning with learning.

Pre and post tests are excellent tools for assessing how much workshop participants have learned during the training process. If the training has been successful at this level, participants have subject matter knowledge they didn't possess at the beginning of the training. Interim written or verbal quizzes for longer workshops, such as one day to a week, can be used to gauge whether participants are absorbing the information. A critical aspect of conducting this type of evaluation, of course, is to be certain that the questions on the tests are on point to the material that must be transferred to the workplace. Trainees that aren't exposed to the knowledge base on a frequent basis starting soon after the training may quickly forget points they remembered on the post test.

Perhaps you've studied a field or area of interest and then tried to apply what you've learned. Linda watched golf tournaments on TV and in person for about three months before she went to a par three course with her new clubs and tried to hit a few balls. Even though she knew that she wasn't supposed to bend her arm at the elbow or grip the club like a baseball bat, Linda didn't have the experience to *execute* what she'd read in the golf digests. You may send trainees to classes on providing positive criticism, yet when a time crunch hits or an extremely challenging assignment comes their way, they revert back to ineffective behaviors prior to the training. We encourage you to take the lead in developing long-term measures of behavior change to assess whether training is truly successful. We'll discuss some of those measures in the next section.

Well-intentioned employees can change their behaviors to appease their managers and customers. Unfortunately, those behavior changes don't always translate to business results that sustain the company's viability. Last year, one of our client organizations took its first-line supervisors through a two-day training on the topic of internal and external customer satisfaction. The focus of the in-house trainer was on asking "why" five times when customers expressed a need for a service or product. The trainer's objective was to ensure that people dug deep to understand the customer's true problems and issues. Not a bad concept.

After a couple of months, outside customers and coworkers began getting annoyed with trainees constantly asking "why" whenever they put in a request. Sometimes, the answer was quite simply, "because this is what I want…and I don't want to have to explain myself." One customer even threatened to stop buying from the company unless sales reps and other staff didn't stop "pestering them" with too many questions! Trainees did change their behaviors; however, the results for the company weren't necessarily positive.

We recommended in chapter 3 that success criteria be established at the beginning of training. These criteria can in turn be used to develop a results-oriented evaluation process, ensuring that the appropriate results are sought.

*Measurement Tools for the Emotionally Intelligent Trainer*

Observation over the long term is a clear indicator of whether a trainee has learned and is executing new competencies or behaviors. Sometimes the trainee's immediate supervisor doesn't know what to look for to gauge whether the expected behaviors are taking place. Trainers with high levels of interpersonal EI will first of all include the trainees' supervisors in the needs assessment process by asking them questions such as, "what do your direct reports need to know how to do that they aren't doing now?" and, "what will the appropriate behavior look like?" If we conduct training on time management, we provide the trainees and their supervisors with clear-cut ways to tell if the training was effective. For example, we might provide a checklist that asks whether trainees turn in priority assignments on time, understand when to ask for assistance, and know when to put a project aside to deal with a more important task. Alternatively, we might review the performance evaluation with the supervisor and point to sections that address time and project management skills.

Another excellent tool to assess long-term results is to conduct surveys or focus groups of people who've been through training events three to six months following the training. Specific questions about the use of tools and techniques covered in the training can be addressed, such as:

- How do you use the Gantt chart technique in your daily work?
- Provide an example of how you've employed situational leadership within the past six months.
- What areas of your work have you transferred to Covey's Quadrant II in the past three months?

We like to provide workshop participants with an action plan at the end of training, such as the one in Appendix 14. An action plan asks participants to identify one or two tasks or projects that they must tackle over the next few weeks or months. Then, the instrument asks the participant to describe how he or she will use one or two of the concepts or tools covered in the training to meet the requirements of the identified tasks. Success criteria are included on the action plan so that, at the end of the assignment, trainees can tell in a concrete way whether they've successfully completed their project.

As a former accountant, Linda can't help from looking at activities and interventions from a return on investment (ROI) perspective. That is, for the time, energy, and money that's invested in an activity, what is the financial return? This example of an intervention to prevent high turnover uses this ROI approach:

*Return on Investment (ROI) Worksheet*

*Step 1.* Clearly state the business problem. For example, our organization has a turnover rate of 32 percent for computer programmers.

*Step 2.* Calculate the cost of the business problem. For example, calculate the turnover costs for separation, replacement, and training for each computer programmer that left the organization in the past year.

*Step 3.* Identify a potential solution to the business problem based on historical data or benchmarking. For example, a study of exit interviews may reveal that key first-line supervisors aren't effective at giving performance feedback. A combination of one-on-one coaching and training may be a viable solution.

*Step 4.* Calculate the cost of the solution. For example, assess the price of having a consultant conduct a series of workshops and the time for an HR staff person to develop and conduct a series of coaching sessions.

*Step 5.* Implement the solution and monitor results. The planned-for result would be lower turnover of computer programmers after three months, six months, a year, and so on, as a result of more effective supervision.

*Step 6.* Calculate the net improvement benefit: Cost of business problem before implementing solution (Step 2)

| | | |
|---|---|---|
| Minus | Savings after intervention, less cost of solution | |
| Example | $585,000 | Annual t/o cost in year 1 |
| | $300,000 | New cost in year 2 |
| | $285,000–$50,000 | Savings, less solution cost |
| | **$235,000** | **Net Improvement Benefit** |

*Step 7.* Calculate the cost-benefit as follows: Net Improvement Benefit (Step 6) ÷ Cost of Solution (Step 4)
$235,000 ÷ $50,000 = 4.7 to 1 (For every $1 spent for the solution, $4.70 was saved). ROI = 4.7 to 1

Organizational leaders want to ensure that investment in trainer time and salary as well as participant time and salary during the training event results in increased revenue or reduced expenses whenever feasible. Sometimes training must be conducted whether or not an immediate financial return is assured. For example, there's often a learning curve when employees are learning a new process or skill. In the short run, some waste or rework might be necessary, and this definitely isn't bringing in dollars! The key is for the trainer to work with trainees and their managers to build in a reinforcement process that builds skills and expertise in as little time as possible so employees can be productive quickly.

*Training Tip*

Be sure to leave a minimum of five minutes at the end of training events for participants to complete feedback instruments. A hastily scribbled evaluation doesn't provide meaningful input. Leave your contact information for participants to contact you after the training so they can provide additional comments.

*Case Study*

Jim is perplexed. He has been conducting in-house training on Effective Communications Skills for first-line supervisors for five years. The evaluations turned in at the end of training have always been pretty good, with occasional negative comments about the length of the training. This morning, he received notice that this workshop and two others that he conducts on a frequent basis are being dropped from the training schedule.

Jim asked his boss, the VP of Human Resources, why his workshops were not going to be continued. The boss responded by saying that the CFO will only approve training that is "value added" and "bottom line oriented." Neither Jim nor his boss is quite sure what those terms mean exactly.

Jim is certain the communications skills workshop should be continued because he often hears comments in the hallways like, "nobody ever listens to me, and I'm going to just quit" and "I have to give a presentation to a customer and I don't know the first thing about PowerPoint." To Jim, it's clear that people want and need his training.

*Discussion Questions*

1. How can Jim determine whether his communications skills training is "value added" and "bottom line oriented"?
2. How can Jim use the suggestions above for the other two workshops he does on a frequent basis?

*Points to Remember*

Having a "gut" feeling that training is effective simply won't impress CFO's, CEO's, and line managers today. Organizational leaders want, and deserve, a concrete answer to the question, "what's in it for the organization to conduct this training?" If Jim and his boss had been providing the answer to this question for his training activities, it's likely they wouldn't have been pulled from the program.

During the needs assessment process, Jim should have asked managers around the organization what specific areas of skill building were necessary for their staff and what—specifically—would successful training do for individuals and their departments. In short, what's the business need or problem? what's the cost of the business problem? how much would training cost? what's the difference between training cost (cost of the solution) and the cost of the problem? If Jim doesn't have historical company data to use, he could research best practices in similar organizations so he could project an ROI. Articles on training best practices and results abound in *HRMagazine*, the monthly publication of the Society of Human Resource Management, and *Training & Development*, the monthly publication of The American Society for Training and Development.

The ROI worksheet can be used for the other training activities Jim is involved with as well.

Jim shouldn't wait for managers and the CFO to come to him for ROI information. He can position training positively by sharing this data with the leadership on an ongoing basis.

The optimal end result of organizational training is improvement in employee performance. Trainers who are tuned in to organizational objectives understand the importance of interacting with all beneficiaries of planned training activities: trainees, trainees' managers, coworkers, executives, external customers, and even shareholders. Appropriate measures for successful training will be different for each of these beneficiaries, and a holistic assessment and measurement process will ensure that the right measures are captured.

# CHAPTER SEVEN

## How to Develop Your Emotional Intelligence as a Trainer

Throughout this book, we've attempted to build a strong case for the advantages of enhancing your emotional intelligence (EI) as a trainer, HRD professional, or leader. The more aware you are of your needs and those of others, the more effective you'll become at assessing situations and taking appropriate actions in response. While this can be a challenging process, developing your EQ can positively affect your life personally and professionally.

In this chapter, we'll share some suggestions for developing EI competencies so that you'll be equipped to achieve excellence as a trainer or leader.

### The Build–A–Bear Concept

Think about your favorite trainer. Why does this person come to mind? Did s/he make a considerable impression upon you? Did s/he really know his/her material and leave you with something you can apply elsewhere? If not, did this trainer at least leave you with an extra "spring in your step" after speaking? Did s/he make you laugh, cry, smile, or just think?

The point is, each person will remember someone different and for a different reason. There is not just one best way to train. There isn't just one right way to train. Each trainer will have their own unique characteristics that will appeal to different participants, for different reasons. Just like the long line of kids waiting patiently to build their bear, with each one choosing different parts to make their bear special, no two bears will ever be the same. Your training style will evolve over time and become yours alone.

### "Building" a Trainer

So, what competencies does an ideal trainer have? If you're already a trainer, you might already have some of the competencies we've previously discussed. However, perhaps your time management skills are poor, or your follow through after training events could be better. Many of us are strong in one or two areas and need help in others. Acceptance is the first step toward positive change, and recognizing that you need assistance or refinement is great. So, if you believe in continuous improvement, keep reading!

Former football coach, motivational speaker, and author Lou Holtz wrote a book entitled *Do the Right Thing*. In this book, Coach Holtz discusses the fact that you don't have to be the best or smartest at something in order to manage it. Often times the shortfall in technical competence can be outweighed by "doing the right thing." We believe that a leader in the training field understands this difference.

James Kouzes and Barry Posner, leadership gurus, have often written about five keys to success as a leader. These include:

1. Modeling how you want others to act on your values
2. Inspiring a shared vision
3. Challenging the usual processes for getting things done by searching for opportunities to innovate
4. Enabling others to act by fostering collaboration and sharing power
5. Encouraging the heart, or recognizing the contributions of others and creating a spirit of community

You hear stories about teams that were the underdog and came from behind to win. Almost always there is a story behind the player or coach who led the team to victory. Going back to Coach Holtz, he was in a position numerous times to play in the big game. His teams were often not the favorite. Yet, when the players were asked how they won, they indicated that it was because of Coach Holtz's inspiration. He led by example and motivated the team by telling them that others didn't feel they should be playing in the big game. He challenged them to get beyond the naysayers and to make them believe in themselves. You can't evolve to this level of leading and inspiring others without EI.

## If You Build It, They Will Come

Getting stakeholders' buy-in and ensuring that they are in agreement about training objectives is critical to success. The buy-in concept applies to the trainer as well. If the trainer doesn't believe in the training, the participants won't either. If the people at the highest levels don't participate in training at least to some degree, others won't see the training as important.

During a recent training session on a new performance appraisal process, one of the company vice-presidents skipped his scheduled training session. In the second session of the day, the company president attended.

Once the word got out that the president attended, the third session was standing room only! The rest of the company realized that this was important once the president participated.

Motivation concepts are important ones for trainers to grasp and use. One key element of motivation theory is that people are motivated differently. In order to get potential participants charged up and energized about a training event, we like to ask them in communications prior to training sessions what *their* expectations and challenges are around the training topic. Once interest levels and key problems are identified, a communication with an abstract of the training can be sent with the agenda and logistics.

We've observed that effective trainers strive to build trust between themselves and participants from the moment people enter the training environment. One way to build trust is to be aware of trainees' "hot buttons," such as issues around compensation levels or position titles. Knowing when to stay away from topics and when to bring them into the conversation is crucial to building trust. When a pattern emerges where participants insist that a tool or idea is not feasible, for example, we like to stop and conduct a Force Field Analysis to surface barriers and support mechanisms. This can allow a positive momentum to take over when several positive aspects of an idea are offered.

As we mentioned earlier, according to Kouzes and Posner, inspiring a shared vision is one of the keys to successful leadership. This concept applies to a classroom as well. Trainers have to empathize with their participants. For instance, trainers may get to go home after a training session; however, the participants will likely have to go back to their desks to complete their day's work. Trainers recognize this and often refer to ways that ideas and techniques will directly help the trainees when they go back to their work stations. Even if a trainer simply acknowledges that work is piling up during the training event, this shows that h/she is aware of the trade-off that trainees are making.

## Walk the Talk

Okay, so you're modeling how you want the others to act, inspiring a shared vision, challenging the status quo, fostering collaboration and sharing power, and recognizing others' accomplishments. You're "doing right" in Coach Holtz's language. Now what?

Becoming a change agent is the next step. This mindset, we want to warn you, is a risky one in many organizations. We encourage you to move forward cautiously, remembering approaches such as Return on Investment to ensure that others buy into your suggested changes.

Perhaps your organization has some poor performers and their managers want to retain them anyway because finding replacements may be time consuming. The managers may believe that the cost of turnover is already high and it's in the best interests of the organization to attempt to turn around poor performance. As a trainer, you may be charged with the responsibility of turning poor performers into effective employees. Your challenge is to take steps to assess the situation and determine, for example, if the true problem is a skill set deficit or inadequate resources, or something else. You may need to speak out and suggest that training is not the best way to address all areas of poor performance. We're suggesting that the trainer will sometimes have to do some homework and suggest other alternatives to training.

Once you understand your role as trainer and the importance of being a change agent, we encourage you to consider your current level of EI, your technical skill set, and your influence within the organization so you know what you can, and cannot, act upon.

A key to increasing EI is recognizing and naming your own feelings. Happiness, Sadness, Anger, Fear, and Shame are the five core emotions described in the literature we've cited throughout our book. You can learn to name your emotions by becoming accustomed to tuning in to the physical signs that accompany feelings. For example, Linda has learned over time to associate clenching her fists with feelings of anxiety. She first became aware of this association when she noticed several pictures of herself over time, in different types of situations, in which she often had her fists clenched. She started to reflect on what was occurring in these pictures and identified several instances in which she was anxious or nervous, even though she had a smile on her face in the pictures.

Ask your friends and family to help you identify your emotional "hot buttons." Accept their feedback and look for these indicators in future interactions. For example, Sheri once had a professor tell her that she didn't accept compliments. He said that it's okay to say thank you instead of telling a person h/she was wrong for giving the compliment. After receiving this feedback, Sheri started to pay attention to her behavior when she received positive comments. She often found herself saying, "Oh, not really," or "It wasn't me," or something other than thank you. From that day on, Sheri began accepting compliments more graciously.

We will sometimes have to receive negative feedback, and that's hard for most of us. Think about the popular television show, American Idol. Simon Cowell, one of the judges, is known for being rude and obnoxious. Often what he says is true; he's just insensitive in his delivery. We've observed that some contestants accept his criticism and even thank him, acknowledging that he's entitled to his opinion. There will undoubtedly be some "Simon Cowells" in our future.

We suggest that you write down those behaviors that allow your emotions to get the best of you, and devise a plan to confront them. For example, perhaps a coworker has left you a nasty phone message after work hours. Instead of responding by phone, plan to confront that person face to face and let him/her know how upsetting the phone call was to you and the importance of resolving the issue. You may find that the person left the message after hours because h/she was uncomfortable with confrontation. You can take a leadership approach and model positive disagreement by demonstrating win–win dialogue. Each incident that you handle in this positive way provides you with experience so you can get past your own feelings of inadequacy in handling confrontations.

We realize that you don't always have time to practice scenarios that might occur. In real life, there are no dress rehearsals. However, the more you reflect on and even practice how you want to approach people, the easier in-the-moment interactions become. For example, in the above phone message example, you could devise a series of questions to help you understand the caller's reasons for leaving the message, such as "Are you upset because the training evaluation summary is late?" Clarification questions like this may lead you to discover that issues you weren't even aware of caused anger or concern. Probe questions help you avoid misinterpreting others' feelings, shows your interest, and help you resolve problems.

Let's shift the focus from training and development to managing emotions as a leader. It may seem unfair; however, those of us in leadership roles are highly visible and vulnerable to open criticism. Given this premise, when you think about people you know who are effective leaders, what attributes come to mind? We've observed that the ability to see a situation realistically and clearly, managing frustration and anger appropriately, and flexibility are key dimensions of EQ that serve leaders well. You may be wondering how to build these dimensions of EQ to be more effective in your own organization.

As we mature and become adults, each of us forms opinions—sometimes very strong opinions—about the world around us. This worldview affects the daily decisions we make as leaders, so it's important to understand how we acquired our perspectives and which ideas are based on facts and which are based on opinions or life's experiences. A good question to ask before making a decision that will affect coworkers, peers, and customers is, "How do I know what I know about what is going to form the basis of my decision?" If your decision is about to be made based on biases, either positive or negative, you must pause and reflect. Perhaps you need more information from reliable sources (that is, coworkers, production data, best practices). A great tool that Linda uses on a regular basis is the Decision Tree Diagram developed by Vroom and Yetton, in figure 7.1 below. This tool helps a leader decide whether he or she has enough information to make a sound decision unilaterally or if coworkers or subordinates should be included in order to have the benefit of as much information as possible.

We were told early in our leadership careers that supervisors aren't allowed to get angry. They're not allowed to be frustrated. They have to just inhale and take everything that comes their way without flinching. We don't believe this is the emotionally intelligent way to manage anger or frustration. There's no doubt that people in leadership positions are held to a high standard when it comes to dealing with, for instance, unfair or untrue criticism or people who aren't committed to keeping their word.

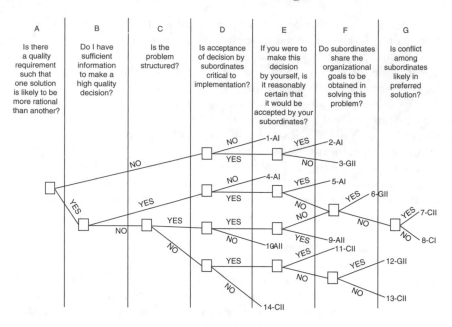

| A | B | C | D | E | F | G |
|---|---|---|---|---|---|---|
| Is there a quality requirement such that one solution is likely to be more rational than another? | Do I have sufficient information to make a high quality decision? | Is the problem structured? | Is acceptance of decision by subordinates critical to implementation? | If you were to make this decision by yourself, is it reasonably certain that it would be accepted by your subordinates? | Do subordinates share the organizational goals to be obtained in solving this problem? | Is conflict among subordinates likely in preferred solution? |

Deciding Who Decides

- A-I: Manager makes decision based upon information already possessed
- A-II: Manager makes decision after receiving information from subordinates
- C-I: Manager makes decision after receiving information and opinions from subordinates one at a time
- C-II: Manager makes decision after receiving information and opinions from subordinates in a group setting
- G-II: Manager becomes a member of group and supports group decision

**Figure 7.1**   Decision Tree

The normal, human response is to get angry and we believe it's alright to acknowledge that emotion to oneself and even to coworkers.

Consider this conversation between a boss and her direct report:

*Boss*: Linda, it's 4:45 and you promised me yesterday that if I gave you another day and took other assignments off your to do list you would have the Widget Report to me by 3:00. It's due to the Board by tomorrow morning at 8:00, and I'd like to review everything before I walk it upstairs.

*Direct Report*: Oh, that's right...you did mention that you needed this by mid-afternoon. Well, you know how the time can just slip away sometimes. I'm still not quite finished, and I guess it'll have to wait since it's almost 5:00 and I leave at 5:00.

*Angry Boss*: Linda, that is simply not acceptable. If you thought earlier in the day that you needed even more assistance with finishing the report, I would have expected you to let me know that immediately. I explained to you more than once the timeline we're under and the importance of this report.

*Direct Report*: I know... I know. I had more interruptions today than I anticipated. If you had stopped by my cubicle and reminded me, maybe I would've remembered to put people off until I finished the report.

*Even-More-Angry Boss*: Linda, when I make an assignment it's your responsibility to complete the work, without my hovering. I have other tasks that I have to take care of every day, and when I delegate a project to you I expect that it will be completed on time.

This is very frustrating for me, and we'll need to talk about how to make sure this is finished and I have an opportunity to review the report before it goes up to the Board at 8:00 in the morning. What do you recommend we do?

*Direct Report*: I guess I can stay for another half hour or so to finish the report. Will that work?

*Calmer Boss*: Yes, that'll work. I'll leave you alone for 30 minutes so you can get this finished.

The boss in this scenario let her direct report know that she was frustrated—as well she should be. Had she exploded, though, the employee might have stormed out, or stayed and worked on the report but been so nervous she couldn't concentrate and do her best work.

The third attribute we believe is important for a leader to build is flexibility. If a person can only operate within a rigid set of procedures and under a set-in-stone time frame, he's going to have countless days of frustration in a leadership role. It may seem like an oxymoron, but we believe that planning is the basis for flexibility. For example, when Linda was called on recently to facilitate an executive meeting for a client organization, she was provided with an end goal and a loose time frame and nothing else in the way of guidance. She needed to have in hand several options for accomplishing the expected end result so she could flex to accommodate each segment of the meeting by using the meeting management technique that would serve the purpose. For instance, she knew that nominal group technique would be a great tool to use if the group ran out of steam and needed an approach to jump start creativity. So she brought post-it notes and left one wall devoid of flip chart pages in the event that technique was required. You can plan to be flexible too. For example, you can think about potential answers to different questions that might be raised during a staff meeting. Even if all the questions don't get raised, you'll have the flexibility to move from point to point—if you've planned ahead.

As Dale Carnegie said, "When dealing with people, remember that you are not dealing with creatures of logic, but creatures of emotion."

Here are some statistics to consider: People experience an average of twenty-seven emotions each waking hour. With nearly seventeen waking hours each day, you have about 456 emotional experiences from the time you get up until the time you go to bed. This means that more than 3,000 emotional reactions guide you through each week and more than 150,000 each year! Of all the emotions you will experience in your lifetime, nearly two million of them will happen during working hours. It's no wonder that people who manage emotions well are easier to work with and more likely to achieve what they set out to do (Bradbery and Greaves, 2005).

*Training Tip*
Not sure what motivates your participants? The long and short answer is the same—just ask them. Who knows better than they do? Why try to guess? It's hard to select something that fits everyone, because we're all different. Even though you may not be able to satisfy all training participants every moment, understanding personal needs across the group will help you in the planning process. In addition, this will help avoid misdirecting valuable time and resources.

*Case Study*
Ann, the Corporate Trainer for Built to Last Homes, was asked by her manager, the VP of HR, to conduct a session on "Giving and Receiving Feedback" for the fourteen managers at the company. Ann thought to herself, "they don't have time for this and they won't want to be there. I'm sure they know how to deliver criticism, and everyone knows the president has yelled at them before, so they must know how to receive the feedback as well." She was afraid this would be a waste of time, but she did as she was directed. She created a session and sent out the schedule inviting the managers to participate. No one RSVP'd, and she ended up receiving criticism of her own from the VP of HR.

*Discussion Questions*
1) What went wrong here?
2) What could Ann have done to determine if the session was needed?
3) Was the scheduling and inviting of the participants done well? What could have been done differently?

*Points to Remember*
1) There are a number of problems with this scenario. First, Ann could have asked the VP of HR why she thought the session was needed. She would then have a better feel for the logic behind the choice of topic and the session timing.

   In addition, Ann jumped to the conclusion that "Giving and Receiving Feedback" was the same as delivering criticism and getting yelled at by the president. She didn't buy into the concept herself, so it was probably hard to convey her excitement about the session in the invitation.

   Of course, the president should not be yelling at his employees, especially in public. If the session is to be well received, the president will need to be in attendance and follow through on changing his behavior.

   The managers could have shared with Ann why they didn't RSVP. Perhaps the day, the timing, the location, the topic, or any combination of these caused the low level of response. Ann cannot know this if she doesn't have feedback.

2) Ann could have asked the VP of HR for more details and then suggested that a needs assessment be conducted. Perhaps people already know how to deliver and receive effective feedback and need assistance in other areas.

3) Ann did not explore timing concerns. She simply selected a date, time, and location without asking for input from potential participants. She could have solicited their support by having them suggest available dates and times.

Ann could have provided incentives for participants, with rewards for attendance. For example, if the session was six hours she could arrange for them to go home early after attending. Especially if the training was on a Friday, people would have lined up to attend!

# CHAPTER EIGHT

# Best Practices from the Best Trainers

After reviewing the survey data from our training specialists, we are confident that the responses received support the topics we've been discussing. Some of the responses clearly came from trainers who exhibit the key components of Emotional Intelligence (EI): Interpersonal Skills, Intrapersonal Skills, Stress Management Abilities, and General Happiness and Positive Attitude. Some responses are at the complete opposite end of the spectrum—from those in need of EI enhancement. This was surprising to us as the responses came from professional trainers and/educators. We were happy to note, however, that for a number of the questions no one selected the response indicating the lowest level of EI.

You will see the survey questions repeated below, with the most given response and the least given response cited, along with the key themes we took away from the respondents' comments. The comments cited are not necessarily right or wrong, but they were large enough in numbers that we felt it was important to report them. The responses demonstrate a range of EI. You will be able to view that range next. We've listed the response that indicates the highest level of EI along with the lowest, and then an average level of EI. This should benefit each reader in that if you take the survey and respond honestly, you'll uncover dimensions of EI you'd like to develop.

1. When conducting a training session, for the initial greeting, I'm most likely to:
   Most given response: Acknowledge people individually after they are seated (37).
   Least given response: Skip the greeting and get to business (0).
   Key Themes from Comments:

- Participants might feel like the "salesperson is coming" if approached at the door.
- A smile or a wave as people enter is sufficient.
- Consider having staff and a registration table outside the meeting room.

Response that Demonstrates EI: Acknowledge people individually after they are seated.

Response that Demonstrates Low Level of EI: Skip the greeting and get to business.

Responses that Demonstrate an Average Level of EI: Stand at the door and greet participants as they enter; Wait to address the entire group together.

Omitting an initial greeting minimizes the trainer's opportunity to bond with the audience and build rapport. Individual acknowledgement might seem like a time waster; however, we found quite the contrary to be true. The personal information a trainer can gain could be an aid during the training, especially after participants are seated and are more comfortable. For example, if a question is asked and no one responds, you would know individuals by name and could call on someone. Also, you might find you have something in common with a participant, and when trying to give an example in your session, you may relate it back to a sports team which that participant supports, or to their particular industry if you discussed their place of employment. The possibilities are endless.

Another common practice is to ask participants to indicate not only their name, but their title, company, and maybe even one expectation they have for the session. Not only will this give you other "small talk" or relatable topics as stated above, you will also be able to enhance your evaluations if you know their expectations upfront and can then be flexible enough to tailor your content to meet or even exceed the participants' expectations.

2. If participants are entering the training room and I'm still preparing flip charts, I am most likely to:
   Most given response: Verbally welcome participants and direct them to refreshments and/or to their seats (29).
   Lease given response: Stop writing on the clip charts and mingle with participants (10).
   Key Themes from Comments:

   • The tone needs to be welcoming and say "I'm glad you're here."
   • Take the opportunity to build rapport with participants early in the process.
   • Do as much prepreparation as feasible so that you appear ready, yet can talk with participants at the beginning.

Response that Demonstrates a High level of EI: Verbally welcome participants and direct them to refreshments and/or to their seats.

Response that Demonstrates a Low level of EI: Focus completely on finishing the flip charts rather than acknowledge individuals as they enter the classroom.

Responses that Demonstrate an Average level of EI: Glance up and smile but continue writing my flip charts; Stop writing on the clip charts and mingle with participants.

The majority of our respondents understood the importance of welcoming the participants to the class and why that is more important than you finishing your flip charts (which should have been completed already) and ignoring them in the process. As stated earlier, it's important to make people feel welcome and acknowledging them can do just that. In addition, if you direct them to their seat and/or refreshments, they won't wonder unnecessarily whether or not it's appropriate to get a beverage.

3. I think ice breakers are:
   Most given response: Dependent on the subject matter as to whether or not they're utilized.
   Least given response: A waste of time.
   Key Themes from Comments:

• Before they're used, consider the audience and the topic for appropriateness.
• Tailor ice breakers to the level of participants.
• Ice breakers might be threatening to some individuals or groups.

Response that Demonstrates a High level of EI: Dependent on the subject matter as to whether or not they're utilized.
Response that Demonstrates a Low level of EI: A waste of time.
Responses that Demonstrate an Average level of EI: Very useful and always good; Semi-useful and used frequently in my training sessions.

Ice breakers can be a huge advantage to getting your class/session started off with a bang! One example is the simple "Name Bingo" that the authors use quite frequently (Appendix 15). Not only does this allow the trainer to learn more about the participants, accomplishing our objective from survey question number one, it also gets the participants involved from the beginning, and creates an energy level in the room that carries on during your training. Students are also less intimidated to participate during the session because they know just about everyone after such an ice breaker and tend to feel more comfortable sharing and/or asking questions.

There are a number of ice breakers, and while they might not seem related to the topic, they can be tied to a concept you might be discussing later in the session. For example, even with the Name Bingo ice breaker just mentioned, the participants are instructed to find someone in the class that matches the item on their bingo card and ask the person to write their name in that box. Once they have a "bingo," they win. Depending on how much time you have, you could also vary this game and ask that they play a "cover all" allowing them to meet everyone in the session. Now, you could have the descriptions in the box related to your topic, for example "Has cried at work" if you're delivering an EI session. Then, during your debrief of the exercise, you can also discuss whether or not anyone involved you as the instructor with this exercise. Often times it just takes one person to ask if any of their items describe you. Others get the drift and soon you have a line to sign one of their bingo boxes. This shows that the first student thought "outside of the box." This creativity can apply to almost any topic you're discussing and is a great segue to your course material.

4. If I'm sharing some information with the class and two people are holding a distracting side conversation, I will probably:
Most given response: Keep talking, but walk over to stand near the area where the sidebar is being held.
Least given response: Talk louder.
Key Themes from Comments:

- The facilitator must handle distractions but in a way that doesn't "turn the crowd" against him or her.
- Set a tone that mutual respect is a ground rule, right from the beginning

Response that Demonstrates a High level of EI: Keep talking, but walk over to stand near the area where the sidebar is being held.
Response that Demonstrates a Low level of EI: Talk louder.
Responses that Demonstrate an Average level of EI: Ignore them; Stop and ask the people who are talking to be quiet.

We believe that trainers should take control of the training environment. Depending on why the participants are attending, trainers may have control over whether they pass the class, or get the promotion/merit increase dependent upon successful completion of the session. Workshop participants can be reminded of objectives and outcomes such as this during the first few minutes of a session. However, it seems that there is always that one participant who wants to "test" trainers. Talking louder doesn't accomplish anything except further annoy the other participants. The same is true with ignoring the disruptive individual. Stopping and asking them to be quiet is also distracting not only to the class who's trying to listen to the trainer, but to the trainer's focus.

We have found an intense stare, along with walking near the person, will often put an end to the sidebar. If that doesn't work, since we've worked hard to build rapport in the beginning of the session, we might call on the disruptive person with a question such as a simple, "What do you think, Kathy?" She will not know how to respond because she wasn't paying attention, but chances of that happening again with anyone in the class now are slim to none.

5. When a training class participant challenges a point I've made, I'm most likely to:
Most given response: Ask the person to express his or her perspective.
Least given response: Defer to the other person's opinion.

Key Themes from Comments:

- If facts are in dispute, point to the facts and gently advise participant of his/her misunderstanding.
- Asking for input from others promotes peer influence, which can be powerful.
- A quality facilitator promotes discussion and respectful disagreement.

Responses that Demonstrate a High level of EI: Ask the person to express his or her perspective.

Response that Demonstrates a Low level of EI: Defer to the other person's opinion.

Responses that Demonstrate an Average level of EI: Tell the person he/she is wrong; Ask for other participants to validate my point.

If you're the "expert," or even perceived to be one based on your position in front of the class, deferring to the other person's opinion will ruin your credibility. However, it is possible that you could be mistaken, and if the other person's point is valid, discussing that further will allow you to explain how perhaps in that particular situation that the participant shared, what is being said is indeed true.

We both have practical as well as classroom experience, and we agree that we don't know it all and will even admit that, but we will always try to generate discussion and if something is in question, we will get back to the person to clarify questions or concerns.

6. When I don't know the answer:
   Most given response: Ask for someone else to respond.
   Least given response: I make up something and pretend I know.
   Key Themes from Comments:

- A strong facilitator promotes sharing and doesn't always have to be the an answer-giver.
- People will know if you try to fake it, sooner or later, then you'll lose credibility.

Response that Demonstrates a High level of EI: Ask for someone else to respond.

Response that Demonstrates a Low level of EI: I make up something and pretend I know.

Responses that Demonstrate an Average level of EI: Admit I don't know; Tell the participants I'll find out the answer and get back to them.

Using the Socratic Method is a huge advantage when you don't know the answer. You can repeat the question, get others to respond, and then based on responses, you may quickly develop an opinion and be able to respond appropriately. If not, as stated in the previous question, you can either admit you don't know all the answers and/or tell the participants you'll research the answer and get back to them.

Again, we both teach at local universities, and much of what we discuss applies in nonunion settings. When someone says, "Yeah, but in a union..." we immediately acknowledge that what we're saying is more applicable to the nonunion setting and see if there are others in the class who want to discuss what might happen in a union setting.

> 7. If the class appears to be bored during the middle of a training session, I usually:
> Most given response: Break participants into discussion groups with a pertinent case study.
> Least given response: Stay on my agenda and hope things improve.
> Key Themes from Comments:

- Wishing and hoping doesn't improve any situation—be proactive.
- If it's been a long day, some humor may help, but don't let the session get away from you.
- A case study or activity that's "real" should help people reenergize.
- If you ask participants what they want to do, they may just leave.

Responses that Demonstrate a High level of EI: Break participants into discussion groups with a pertinent case study.

Response that Demonstrates a Low level of EI: Stay on my agenda and hope things improve.

Responses that Demonstrate an Average level of EI: Take five minutes out and tell some jokes; ask participants what they'd rather do.

Humor is so subjective, you run a risk when you tell any joke as to whether they'll "get it" and then whether or not they'll think it's funny. Of course, politics and religion are two subjects to stay away from, but to lighten the tension, you could say something they'd never expect. For example, a fellow professor was getting ready to start her Training and Development class with a group of undergraduate seniors in their last semester, who really just wanted the class to be over; sensing their nervousness, she walked over to the piano in the classroom (adjunct professors get put in just about any classroom that's available) and sat down as if she were going to play. She said, "everyone is here for music class, right?" The class laughed and one participant started calling out requests. The class continued to laugh, and now she had their attention. That's an example where humor worked. If it doesn't work, you now have a longer haul ahead of you than before you told the joke. An important dimension of EI is the ability to "read the room" and adapt to the mode appropriately.

Another dimension of EI revolves around being perceptive and aware of facial expressions and knowing when those expressions indicate it's necessary to stray from the agenda. Nothing could be worse than sticking to the agenda "no matter what," even though participants are distracted by something that was said earlier. This applies to team meetings as well as training environments. Linda was facilitating a process improvement team the same day that a memo came out in the company about employee benefits being changed. Many employees didn't understand the memo and thought their benefits were being taken away. This was a hot topic of discussion as Linda began facilitating the meeting, and she noticed right away that team members weren't focused. They were still worried about the benefits memo. So she called a break and asked the Human Resources Director if she could take a few minutes to come to the meeting, clarify the memo, and address questions. Was this a waste of meeting time? Absolutely not. In fifteen minutes, peoples' questions were addressed and they could focus on the topic for the rest of the meeting.

We've found that most adult learners like to be involved and active in the learning process. A very effective way to get the learners engaged is to put them into small groups and give them a case study. If it's based on a real situation, that's even better. Ask them to discuss the case, and get their opinion on how to handle the situation. This allows for those who would not normally speak in front of the whole class to "warm up" in a small group setting, and it also allows for them to brainstorm and toss around various ideas, looking for the best one to present to you and the class. Now, their minds are working and they should be more engaged.

8. During a whole-group discussion about a seemingly benign topic, a workshop participant bursts into tears. You are most likely to:
   Most given response: Call a short break and talk to the person to see if you can assist.
   Least given response: Ignore the situation.
   Key Themes from Comments:

   • You don't need to diagnose the problem, but you should demonstrate that you care about the individual (see what's going on so you can decide the next step).
   • This situation would distract others if it's ignored.

Response that Demonstrates a High level of EI: Call a short break and talk to the person to see if you can assist.
Response that Demonstrates a Low level of EI: Ignore the situation.
Responses that Demonstrate an Average level of EI: Call a ten-minute break so the person can calm down; tell the person he/she may be excused to pull him/herself together.

The problem won't go away if it isn't addressed, so instead of ignoring it, it's better to call a short break. By talking to the person and offering assistance, it shows you care, and while you may not be able to fix the situation, it will go a long way with not only the person to whom you offered help, but also to the class—again to show empathy, which is a dimension of Interpersonal Skills.

9. When a session runs longer or shorter than planned, I will:
   Most given response: Finish on time but assign "homework" whether it be in class or at home.
   Least given response: Ensure the agenda is completed regardless of time.
   Key themes from Comments:

- Participants are mentally gone after the publicized stop time; don't try to go on.
- It's important to cover mutually agreed on material; do process checks periodically to discover what those points are.
- Agendas are like some rules—meant to be broken.

Response that Demonstrates a High level of EI: Finish on time but assign "homework" whether it be in class or at home.

Response that Demonstrates a Low level of EI: Move to the next subject even if it's a day early or late.

Responses that Demonstrate an Average level of EI: Ensure the agenda is completed regardless of time; add "fluff" to fill time or cut out irrelevant information to shorten the session.

Again, recognizing the signs from your learners will help you stick to your time schedule and not necessarily your agenda. An empathetic trainer is perceptive to the learners' needs and adjusts accordingly. While cutting irrelevant information to shorten the session is a good idea, irrelevant information shouldn't have been included in the first place. The same is true with "fluff." The participants are perceptive, so if you're adding unrelated material, they will not benefit from that and will only resent you keeping them longer than necessary. In fact, almost everyone enjoys finishing anything early, so why not let them out when you're finished rather than to keep them "engaged," assign homework that they can do either at the end of the session or truly at home and bring back to discuss further the following session, if appropriate. If the session is over, there's always follow-up by phone or e-mail, so give it a try.

10. If something goes wrong, such as the room not being set up or the time is changed or the training materials are missing, I normally will:
    Most given response: Move to "Plan B" and do a different activity.
    Least given response: Cancel the session.
    Key Themes from Comments:

- Flexibility is critical; go in with contingency plans.
- A session is better rescheduled than be of poor quality.

Response that Demonstrates a High level of EI: Move to "Plan B" and do a different activity.

Response that Demonstrates a Low level of EI: Cancel the session.

Responses that Demonstrate an Average level of EI: Ad lib; postpone and reschedule the session.

Regardless of your profession, you should always have a Plan B! In our MAD world, that is one of Mergers, Acquisitions, and Divestitures, all levels of employees need a backup plan should their company be bought or sold. It never hurts to have a current resume. The same is true with education and training. Sheri arrived at her Human Resources' classroom and distributed the syllabus, and to her surprise, she finds that half the class was there for chemistry. The HR classroom had been changed, so Sheri and half the class proceeded to the new classroom, while the remaining chemistry students waited for their professor. With a good amount of time "wasted," Sheri altered her plans for that evening's session, just covering the syllabus and delaying the discussion of the first chapter.

Another situation pertained to a group who was ready to deliver their group project to their class. Since they hadn't checked the classroom equipment in advance, they had the wrong media and had to ad lib without having backup notes or even transparency slides. This was after a lot of preparation on the written portion of the project, not to mention dress rehearsals of the verbal portion of the project, all for naught when they found out that the equipment was not compatible. Again, checking things such as room assignment and computer equipment in advance is a wise move, and even then, equipment could break, so it's best to have a Plan B.

11. As a trainer, my thoughts on continuous learning to shore up my knowledge base are:

    Most given response: I'm careful with who/where I accept information.

    Least given response: I'm the trainer, so I'm already the expert and don't need to learn more.

    Key Themes from Comments:

- Take a planned, strategic approach to ongoing learning—be current on key issues that affect your organization and its success.
- Be selective about resources; retain cutting-edge knowledge.

Response that Demonstrates a High level of EI: I'm always open to learning more.

Response that Demonstrates a Low level of EI: I'm the trainer, so I'm already the expert and don't need to learn more.

Responses that Demonstrate an Average level of EI: I'm careful with who/where I accept information; it's nice to know, yet it's not practical for me to continually update my training materials.

This is the first survey question where the majority of respondents did not select the response indicating the highest level of EI. A component of EI is curiosity about people, places, and events. As stated earlier, none of us ever know it all, and things are constantly changing, so it's smart to stay current and learn as much as possible about your subject, whether it's from your peers, white papers, or even the Internet. The same is true with organizations. Companies that are willing to invest in the development of their employees recognize that it's better to train them and provide them with the information to help the company advance instead of losing them to the competition. This type of company is known as a "learning organization." Those working in a learning organization will respond to the question, "But what if we train them and they leave?" with a simple, "What if you don't train them and they *stay*?"

We were surprised that most of the respondents were extremely cautious about their sources of information. In our follow-up, we discovered that they've been "burned" before and were provided with incorrect information. That being said, instead of running with the first piece of information you receive, try a new approach and look to disprove what you just learned. Often in this "Devil's Advocate" process, you'll come across an additional source of information either agreeing with what you just learned or discounting that information you acquired.

Lastly, while it might not be practical for you to invest the hours required in order to stay current in your field, you can always get updates from your local professional associations or membership groups. For example, each of us belongs to our local Society for Human Resource Management chapter, and in Toledo, for example, legislative updates are given at the monthly meetings. A local attorney thoroughly reads and interprets any new legislation impacting the field of HR, and he provides a short, concise update to the membership. With new laws being implemented just about every week, it would be virtually impossible for the practitioner to stay current. By being a Toledo Area Human Resource Area (TAHRA) member, for example, coauthor Caldwell is able to stay current by allowing one hour per month to attend her local chapter meetings.

12. With respect to revising training materials, I try to tweak my training programs:
    Most given response: Every time I use them.
    Least given response: Only when I'm told.
    Key Themes from Comments:

    • Updating materials keeps me current and fresh in my thinking.
    • Practically speaking, if you do frequent training, you can't update every time.
    • Keep abreast of and include changes, such as new laws or regulations.

Response that Demonstrates a High level of EI: Every time I use them.

Response that Demonstrates a Low level of EI: Only when I'm told.
Responses that Demonstrate an Average level of EI: Once every year; rarely, if ever.

As stated in the key themes from this question's comments, if you're training frequently, it's impractical to think that you could update your materials every time you use them. In that case, an annual update is a decent alternative. However, many of the trainers we surveyed did not face this situation and recommended updating the materials every time they're used. This does allow for the most current information to be presented. Almost every topic you're delivering will look stale if you're sharing "old" information.

For example, if you're delivering a class on training technology, you'd look silly to discuss using the overhead projector and transparencies (although they could be a good back up plan if the newest technology isn't working) when there are so many more current, advanced ways of learning.

13. What process do you use to prepare for a training session whether you have or haven't worked with the group before?
    Most given response: I meet with some of the actual participants.
    Least given response: I don't meet with anyone in advance.
    Key Themes from Comments:

  • The participants' supervisors aren't always aware of their direct reports' needs.
  • A profile of participants in advance helps me prepare better.

Response that Demonstrates a High level of EI: I meet with some of the actual participants.
Response that Demonstrates a Low level of EI: I don't meet with anyone in advance.
Responses that Demonstrate an Average level of EI: I meet with the training coordinator; I meet with the supervisor of the attendees.

If possible, it's best to meet with the actual participants in advance, as that will give you the extra information discussed in question one about addressing participants once they've been seated. In fact, these two suggestions tie nicely together. If you're able to meet with the participants in advance, even through e-mail, you now have that connection and just need to put a name with a face.

A worthwhile alternative is to meet with the training coordinator, if applicable, and/or the attendees' supervisors. This advance knowledge can alert you to any potential issues, such as reluctant attendees, or even trouble makers. In addition, you can also learn the supervisor's expectations and be sure to include those goals as your objectives.

In the popular reality TV show, The Apprentice, two teams are given a task each week, and the team that meets with the project lead gets the "inside scoop" of what they'd like to see as the final product. The team that doesn't meet with the person in charge of "voting" usually loses. Inevitably, they miss a crucial piece of information. Therefore, ultimately, success is tied to exceeding expectations, on time, and under budget. In other words, under-promise and over-deliver, not the opposite.

14. To measure the results of your training, what method do you use the most?

    Most given response: Actual data such as volume, profitability, or quantity.

    Least given responses: A survey as soon as the session is complete to assess their feelings about the content, the setting, and myself; A test to ensure they understand the material just presented.

    Key Themes from Comments:

- Training must first and foremost be aligned with strategic objectives: that's the success criteria.
- The ROI approach to training is significant and lends credibility to training activities.

Response that Demonstrates a High level of EI: Actual data such as volume, profitability, or quantity.

Responses that Demonstrate a Low level of EI: A survey as soon as the session is complete to assess their feelings about the content, the setting, and myself; a test to ensure they understand the material just presented.

Response that Demonstrates an Average level of EI: Observation to see first hand their newly acquired behavior in action.

This question was the only one where the lower level EI response tied with one response of an average level of EI. This question connects to Kirkpatrick's levels of evaluation: Reaction, Learning, Behavior, and Results. The Reactionary level is the lowest level, just as in our measurement of EI, because as most people realize, a survey can be impacted by so many unrelated factors. If the food was uncooked or the room was too cold, the survey will most likely be poorer than if the food was fantastic and the temperature was perfect. Moving up Kirkpatrick's scale, Learning can be measured by a test, which is good, although they may have had the knowledge prior to your session, and observation is even better than a test, since their behavior can be seen first hand. Unfortunately, the Hawthorne Effect can come into play and performance can be enhanced due to being observed, and it may diminish once no one is paying attention. Therefore, the best way to measure success of training is with Results, which is Kirkpatrick's highest level. Practically speaking, from a training perspective, this is also the most difficult measurement. However, showing the Return on the Investment (ROI) can help insure credibility and stability for the training provider/educator.

Try to determine what criteria will indicate success up front; for example, if you're looking for increased productivity that is easily measured and the quantity and quality levels can be predetermined. Sheri had a training session on Negotiations at her company. The trainer guaranteed that the company would recoup their training fee with the techniques he'd share, within three months, but the employees would have to keep a track every time they negotiated a better deal each month. Surprisingly, within one month, the employees had saved more than double the trainer's fee. Was the training successful? You bet! Could we show the ROI? Absolutely. Enough said.

15. Who has been the biggest obstacle you've had to overcome with respect to gaining "buy in"?
    Most given response: Direct supervisors or line managers.
    Least given response: Participants themselves.
    Key Themes from Comments:

    • Frontline supervisors have a significant impact on whether trainees employ tools and techniques that were learned.
    • There's some trickle-down effect from top levels if training is truly supported.
    • If participants help set training objectives, they buy in much quicker.

Response that Demonstrates a High level of EI: Direct supervisors or line managers.

Response that Demonstrates a Low level of EI: Participants themselves.

Responses that Demonstrate an Average level of EI: Top management, executives, CEO/president level leadership; coworkers of those being trained.

It's refreshing that most participants didn't have trouble getting a buy-in from the top levels nor from the participants or their peers, and usually these levels of people understand that, in the end, the additional training being provided is for the best. While it may be a short-term loss in that the trainee is actually away from the workplace during training, the long-term gain outweighs this loss. Unfortunately, the participant's direct boss is often the roadblock because they desperately need the person to be working, not in training. This shortsightedness can usually be overcome when the actual results are shared, which again is another reason that aiming for Kirkpatrick's highest level of evaluation is recommended. It's hard to discount logic. One other roadblock participants often face, however, is when they're back "on the job" and doing things the way they were taught in training. It may be taking them a little bit longer than normal, as is the case with many newly acquired skills. In general, if someone is not going to support things being done the newer, slower way in the short term, that's going to be the direct supervisor. The training then becomes a waste of time as the skill isn't transferred from the classroom to the job site, if it's not supported. Again, the "proof is in the pudding," so the best way to overcome this lack of support is to show evidence of how this supervisor will gain productivity, for example, if he/she supports his worker while the new skill is implemented. In the end, the results can normally convey greater success and the line manger will likely be more understanding and cooperative.

We believe that trainers and supervisors will benefit from being pro-active, getting any information and support they can up front, having a Plan B (just in case), allowing expression and thinking out of the box, being flexible and altering plans if necessary, being willing to continuously learn, understanding the need and the expectations, and delivering what's needed to show the end results.

# CHAPTER NINE

# Leadership Practices: A Framework for Success

The Global Leadership Forecast Study 2008/2009 (*Global Leadership Forecast 2008/2009*, Executive Summary, Howard and Wellins) reveals an interesting study by Development Dimensions International (DDI), a global workforce and leadership training, staffing, and assessment firm based in Bridgeville, PA. This study indicates that companies are at risk of losing a substantial number of their executives within the next five years. The study also states that 75 percent of executives surveyed for the *Global Leadership Forecast 2008/2009 identified improving or leveraging their* leadership talent as a top business priority. Yet, despite recognition of its importance, leadership development is going nowhere fast. Currently, most leaders are not satisfied with their organization's development offerings. Confidence in leaders has also steadily declined since 2000.

Companies are faced not only with the challenge of replacing existing managers, but as the population continues to age and Baby Boomers leave the workplace, the recent need is to add new managers, according to a recent hiring survey conducted by Management Recruiters International, Inc., one of the largest and most successful recruitment organizations in the world (with 1000 offices in more than thirty-five countries).

In fact, more than half of the companies surveyed indicated they are planning staffing increases at the management levels. In our own survey research, 23 percent of companies surveyed have a structured plan for leadership continuity. We believe that U.S. organizations will begin to pay more attention to leadership continuity over the next decade, if for no other reason than the fact that there are fewer Gen Xers in the population to take the place of retiring Boomers. Organizations will have to be competitive for quality employees, and succession planning grabs the attention of Gen Xers and Generation Next. We also found a positive correlation between training participants viewing training activities as practical and useful and the existence of a publicized succession plan. From both the organizational and individual standpoint then, a plan for leadership continuity makes sense.

When we refer to succession planning in this chapter, we're thinking of a systematic approach toward ensuring there's sufficient "bench strength" at any given time with the skills, knowledge, and abilities to lead the organization. Succession planning is, in many respects, a numbers game. It is an analytical process that requires good organizational skills, attention to detail, and the ability to project into the future. In our surveyed organizations, critical elements of a succession plan include:

- Identification of High Potential Candidates.
- Structured Mentor Initiatives.
- Directed Developmental Assignments.
- Specific Success Criteria and Measurements.

We have found in our work over the past several years that there are five drivers for success in a leadership continuity process:

1. Top Leadership Involvement.
2. Design Creativity.
3. Defined Success Criteria.
4. Identification of Core Leadership Competencies.
5. Clear Communication to Stakeholders.

Top executives must do more than give "lip service" to succession planning. To be successful, a succession plan needs "teeth." In other words, key people within the organization must be champions for leadership continuity and take part in identifying the core competencies necessary to achieve the company's mission and vision. If the company requires directors and managers to participate in multi-rater feedback, executives need to take the lead in soliciting this type of feedback themselves. As top executives model core competencies, people at all levels within the organization see firsthand what is necessary to ensure organizational resiliency.

Sheri's former boss used to tell her that she couldn't advance (or leave) until her replacement was trained to fill her role. Talk about motivation to fully train your subordinates! Upper management needs to hold all managers accountable for identifying talent among their staff. This means that they need to extend themselves to learn as much as possible about others, which is a key dimension of Emotional Intelligence.

A succession plan that works for IBM will not necessarily work for every company, so plan developers must be creative in designing a unique, tailored plan to fit their organization's parameters. Options for career growth need to be practicable within the industry and tailored to the current size of the company; however, other options besides a linear, upwardly mobile pattern should be created. Lateral moves within many organizations can provide as much challenge and growth potential as promotions.

For example, in banking, it is very common to have a designated leader go through a management rotation in every department to learn more about each field and function and ultimately be assigned to one area, and thus be better equipped to succeed with knowledge of every aspect of the business.

The same is true with many family businesses. At Sargento, for example, the family met early on to determine who would run the business after the current President, a second generation Sargento, announced that he planned to retire in five years. There were four sons from whom to choose a successor. A battery of tests, many assessments, and interviews were conducted by an independent, third-party expert in the field of psychology. One of the sons was identified as the heir apparent. He then began a one- to two-year rotation in every department, spending time in Sales/Marketing, Accounting/Finance, Information Systems/Human Resources, and Supply Chain. Upon completion of this rotation, he will be fully trained to continue the successful leadership of the cheese corporation.

In our researched organizations, the method most often used to determine individuals' succession to higher level positions is "proven skills and competencies." We believe that a defined success criteria such as this should be established at the outset, as well as a success criteria for the succession plan as a whole. For example, executives should ask themselves:

- Will we fill gaps with outside talent or will we develop our existing staff?
- Do we want a succession plan to attract target segments of the workforce?
- Will our succession plan be developed to assist us in creating a mentorship culture?
- Do we expect our succession plan to improve retention of staff at specific levels in the organization?
- What core competencies do we require for people in positions at the first-line supervisor, mid-manager, and director level?
- Are we prepared to invest not only time but the necessary dollars to get the designated leader the training required to advance?

One of Linda's clients recently initiated a leadership continuity process, and the identified high potential candidates have been asked to take the EQ-i self-assessment. The EQ-i will provide the candidates with an understanding of the dimensions of EQ that are out of balance and are therefore an opportunity for growth for inclusion in their Individual Development Plan (IDP). One of the high potential employees, for instance, is technically very skilled; however, she has difficulty reading coworkers' confusion when she is explaining highly technical material one-on-one or in a classroom setting. The self-assessment highlighted this challenge so she can take specific steps to shore up her verbal communication abilities.

Stakeholders in the leadership continuity process may include potential leaders, the organization's Board, potential mentors, and existing top executives. As a succession plan is being designed and implemented, each of these stakeholders must be kept informed about their role and how they can benefit from staying involved and committed to the process.

As with any organization-wide initiative, several factors can become impediments to success. The factors that we've seen derail succession plans include:

- No differentiation between high performers and high potential employees.
- Lower morale for employees not selected as "hi pos."
- Underestimating the talent within the organization.
- Focusing exclusively on hard skills.
- Failure to establish process checkpoints.
- Absence of a process champion.
- Keeping the plan a secret.
- Not holding managers accountable.
- Impatience and the desire to pull the "hi po" from his or her training assignment.

We are characterizing high performing employees as those who are doing a better than average job in their current assignments, yet aren't willing or interested in moving throughout the organization to take on lateral or higher level assignments. For example, a person serving as an Accounts Payable Clerk may be doing an excellent job in this role but not be interested in returning to college to obtain a Bachelor's Degree in order to move into a managerial position and/or work extra hours often required in a higher level position. A high potential employee, on the other hand, is a person who is willing and able to take on directed assignments, enroll in additional educational opportunities, and take the extra personal time necessary to increase skills and competencies. Both types of individuals are crucial to an organization's success.

Organizations are finding that EI is a critical factor in determining the success of high performers and high potentials, even further, soft skills, such as EI, are often more important in determining an employee's success than the more traditional hard skills or technical abilities that we tend to value.

Linda often coaches new executives in building components of their EI that are out of balance. On EI assessments such as the EQ-i, high scores across the board aren't the objective. Balanced scores are most meaningful in determining executives' success.

For instance, one recent coaching client of Linda's scored very high in the dimension of assertiveness, an interpersonal component of EI. Unfortunately, he scored lower than the norm in the dimension of empathy, which meant that he had a tendency to push his ideas and beliefs onto coworkers and staff without trying to understand their perspectives and feelings. Until Linda could make him aware that he was losing respect from coworkers, he was blissfully unaware that he was not well liked and people generally avoided spending time with him. This factor was definitely holding him back as a potential top executive.

If your organization has individuals who are technically competent and show promise, we encourage you to consider the EQ-i to uncover dimensions of EI that can be enhanced in order to ensure their success. Consider organizational culture and teamwork needs in addition to technical requirements when building your plan.

We highly recommend that the succession plan be communicated and that career planning and development opportunities be made available for both the high performers and the "hi pos" in order to sustain the morale and high motivation level of all employees. Both types of employees deserve the training described throughout this book. The outcomes of the training activities will simply be different, depending on the track selected. The more you can involve the entire organization in your efforts, the more successful you will be. How many promising employees do you think you've lost to competitors because they had no idea you had them in your sights as "promising"?

One manager told us of her "A list." This is her own version of a "little black book" with all the names and contact information of those "hi pos" she's come in contact with, whether as a colleague, a business associate, or even an interviewee. She said she will even tell someone that she's adding them to her "A list" so that when the right opportunity comes along, she'll have their contact information handy and can make a connection. She said it's amazing how well that works. Her coworkers tell her that they just remember the good ones, but when it comes down to it, there are a lot of "good ones" out there and it's easy to forget without an "A list."

Even the most eloquent succession plans can veer off course without attention and nurturing. In its design phase, we suggest that process checkpoints are built into the process to ensure that outcomes are measured against objectives at least two or three times a year. If barriers have surfaced to impede success, these barriers can be addressed by the process champion, a person highly placed within the organization who can "move heaven and earth" to make important work happen. The process champion collaborates with the process owner (often Human Resources or Organizational Development) to ensure that tactics are in place to sustain the process over time.

You may find that your existing managerial staff feels threatened when asked to identify their successor. If so, we recommend that you tie their pay and/or promotional opportunities to their success in identifying and/or developing the talent within their group. While talking with a vice-president at an international company, we learned that his managers needed to consider the future potential of every new hire and/or promotion. In order for the managers to advance, they needed to have a replacement ready to go. He shared one example in which he complimented his HR Leader for presenting a very strong candidate to fill a generalist opening. On paper, she appeared more experienced than the manager/boss presenting her. In their culture, managers aren't intimidated by hiring the "cream of the crop." Actually, the company has found that the managers are motivated by their own advancement opportunities, and in return they are getting higher quality candidates.

We also believe that managers need to be cognizant of the talent within an organization instead of choosing to automatically recruit from a vast pool of unknowns. An old management credo says, "An expert is someone who lives 50 miles away and carries a briefcase." Consider how many of your employees may be considered expert by the competition in the next town (or on the next block). Do you really want to risk losing them?

If you're in human resources, we think it's a good idea to reflect on whether all systems are "go" prior to launching a succession plan. Are internal and external recruitment and selection processes in place? Is there a rewards and recognition system that is aligned with the objectives of the succession plan? Is an HRIS system in place to track each "hi pos" success? If not, this needs attention prior to the launch. We have two tools that may help in your development efforts: a sample competency-based job description (Appendix 16)and a sample career matrix (Appendix 17). The competency-based job description includes a specific description of behaviors required to achieve the tasks and functions listed. This type of job description answers the question, "what does success look like?" The career matrix describes competencies such as communications across levels in a job family, so employees who aspire toward career development can see in a glance the degree of sophistication required for each required competency the higher they go in the organization.

Linda has successfully employed the process described below over the past several years in assisting organizations establish and enhance their leadership continuity initiatives.

## Succession Planning Process

1. *Leadership Development is Set as a Core Objective.* Top leadership commits to establishing, implementing, and maintaining an ongoing leadership development process that will develop the skills, knowledge, attitude, and abilities of current and future leaders in order to ensure the organization survives and thrives. This can't be done in a vacuum. How can you ensure this happens? Build a solid business case with both internal and external data. Such external data is available through the Bureau of Labor Statistics (BLS) and when combined with your internal statistics a solid succession plan case can be established.

2. *Determine Outcomes, Communications Method, and Metrics.* Top leadership needs to have a vision and address the question, "what does success look like?" Metrics are established that clearly represent success in the near and long term. When and how the process should be communicated to staff at all levels is determined.

3. *Identify Critical Positions for Succession Planning.* Top leadership decides whether to establish "bench strength" for executive positions only or integrate the process to Director and Manager levels. An accurate understanding of your existing workforce, who's eligible for retirement within the next five years, and whether or not any of your people might be ready, willing, and able to step into those positions must be made. Do you have this information "in your head" or in a database accessible at will by anyone with the "need to know"?

4. *Succession Planning Set as Goals for Senior Managers.* The performance review process for senior managers includes metrics identified in step #2 so that all senior managers understand expectations and are invested in succession planning, perhaps even tying such results to their bonuses, if applicable.

Note: For both Steps 3 and 4 above, never assume a key position is safe. For example, if one of the key positions for your organization is that of quality control manager, and the incumbent is a very loyal thirty-something who you feel "will be with the company forever," you may feel that slot is "safe." That's a dangerous assumption. As difficult as it may be, you need to realize that your loyal employee could always be lured to another job, could decide that corporate life is no longer what s/he wants or, even more tragically, could die or become disabled and unable to fulfill the requirements of the position. Anything could happen, so you need a backup plan.

1. *Identify Core Leadership Competencies.* Top leadership brainstorms five to eight core competencies (such as innovation and decision making) that are necessary for targeted positions. The competencies are reduced to writing, with specificity around behaviors for each competency. As you examine your workforce, stay objective, focusing on the core competencies for the *key positions*, regardless of the traits of the incumbents

2. *Create Position Profiles.* Competency-based profiles (job descriptions) are developed for each of the targeted positions.

3. *Differentiate Between High Potentials and High Performers.* Top leadership identifies potential candidates for succession based on their current ability, potential, and willingness to take developmental steps required to achieve the desired competency level. Keep an open mind in this process. Too often succession planning focuses on "the cream of the crop"—those employees who, for whatever reasons, can clearly and readily be identified as "up and comers." You're limiting your potential if you stop with these employees, however. Sometimes, hidden talents can be found in the most retiring or "invisible" workers.

4. *Integrated Key Talent Review Session.* Top leadership meets to candidly discuss known internal and external candidates with potential to succeed in target positions. The discussion should include reflection on critical dimensions of EI that candidates may need developed; that is, interpersonal skills, intrapersonal skills, or stress management.

5. *Develop a List of Potential Directed Assignments.* A list of short-term and long-term assignments and projects that will provide experience and skill building for specified competencies is developed.

6. *Communicate Commitment for Development to High Potential Candidates.* If the top leadership elects to communicate to "hi pos" their status, meet with identified individuals to share the objectives of the succession plan and ascertain their interest in pursuing a career track. Don't keep the plan a secret. Educate the other staff members as well so they too understand the gaps and are in a better position to raise their hand, if interested.

7. *Multi-Rater Feedback.* Develop, administer, and assess the results of multi-rater feedback for identified high potential candidates, as well as individuals in top level positions. Decide whether to utilize an external consultant for this process.

8. *Determine Individual and Organizational Leadership Gaps.* Synthesize the results of the multi-rater process to determine which competencies require development, both for individuals and for the leadership team as a whole.

If your organization determines that it will need employees who are skilled in outside sales and determines that this talent does not currently exist, you are left with two choices: recruit talent from the outside or develop opportunities for interested existing staff with identified potential to learn the skills they will need. Once the gaps have been identified, the next step is to determine how those gaps will be filled either through recruitment or development of existing staff. Development activities might involve in-house training, special project assignments, or outside coursework.

9. *Create Individual Development Plans (IDPs).* Create IDPs for each individual participating in the process, to include directed assignments, ongoing education, workshops, and mentoring. The foundation for these plans can include recent performance reviews, results from multi-rater feedback, and results of an EI assessment such as the EQ-i.

10. Roll Up of Multi-Rater Feedback and Executive Interviews. Share results of multi-rater feedback and EI assessments with individuals and discuss the IDPs. Add additional viable suggestions for development recommended by individuals.

11. Implement Individual Development Plans and Review Semiannually. This is not a one size fits all plan. Step back and allow individuals and their mentors to execute their specific action plans. Provide ongoing unofficial feedback and structured semiannual reviews.

12. Create Leadership Development Curriculum. If the organization wishes to have an internal Learning Institute, work with a consultant well versed in curriculum development to ensure programs are in place as individuals have need of them in their IDP process.

13. Review HR Systems for Alignment. Ensure that Human Resource Management structures are in place for performance management, compensation, and benefits.

14. Quarterly Checkpoint Meeting. Top leadership meets quarterly to assess whether success criteria are being met and consider what barriers may exist that are hindering success, and develop action steps to remove the barriers. It can be tempting to overlook the need for succession planning in the face of more immediate needs. So, quarterly meetings keep the top management involved and ensures that it has the necessary ongoing attention and action that it deserves.

15. Annual Talent Review Discussion. Top leadership meets to assess where high potential candidates are in terms of identified success criteria. The process is fine-tuned to meet the changing environment. High performing employees are reassessed to determine if their situation has changed.

16. Measure Results. This is an ongoing process. Top leadership assesses whether specified objectives, such as reduced turnover of quality staff, are being met.

---

*Tools to Identify High Potential Employees*
Some of the same tools that we've mentioned in chapter 4 will help organizations identify high potential employees. Many of the characteristics of emotionally intelligent trainers exist in emotionally intelligent leaders. For example, in their book titled *Resonant Leadership*, Boyatzis and McKee include self-awareness, self-management, social awareness, and relationship management as competencies critical for leadership success.

Many organizations with whom we've worked employ a multi-rater feedback process to help aspiring leaders determine their level of competencies in areas such as those mentioned above. Appendix 6 contains a multi-rater instrument that we've developed and captures critical leadership competencies.

Other tools that your organization might want to consider for determining competence levels for "hi pos" are self-evaluations, focus groups, and one-on-one interviews with employees who work closely with these candidates.

CHAPTER TEN

# Enhancing Key Dimensions of Your Emotional Intelligence

Regardless of our organizational role, each of us has the ability to enhance our Emotional Intelligence (EI)! In this chapter, we'll recommend ways that individuals can supplement innate verbal, logical, visual/spatial, intrapersonal, and interpersonal elements of EI. And unlike the commercials, we do encourage you to "try this at home!"

## Ways to Enhance Verbal Abilities

Do you ever find yourself searching for just the right word, either when writing a letter or explaining how you feel about an issue? To expand your vocabulary, the Thesaurus can be your new best friend. In many word processing software programs, a Thesaurus is included in the Tools section of the menu. Take a minute when you're composing to look up words that are the best fit for your intended meaning. If you're about to make a presentation, whether it's for a conference or an internal staff meeting, pull out a hard copy of a Thesaurus and check for similar words to those you're considering but aren't completely satisfied are exactly right.

For some people, daily journaling is cathartic and a wonderful way to capture thoughts, impressions, and reactions to one's everyday existence. If you haven't ever kept a journal, consider starting one. This is a terrific—and private—way to become accustomed to using the written word as a means of personal expression. Stationery stores offer a wide selection of journals, from the basic notes pages style to hardbound fancier styles. The cover isn't what's important—the opportunity to capture your thoughts, hopes, and dreams in writing is empowering.

If you'd prefer, you can tailor the concept of journaling to your workplace. For instance, you can write specifically about what you accomplish at the end of each day, and actions that were productive or nonproductive. You can write down a draft script of a conversation you'd like to have with a coworker or your boss. Writing, and then reflecting on what you've written, can help you expand both your vocabulary and your approach toward interacting with others.

Some of you might be wondering if you could write a book, or at least a journal article, or a chapter in a book. We can say that our grasp of the language has certainly been enhanced as a result of writing this book! For instance, Linda is very sensitive to over- using a word or a phrase. In order not to be repetitive, she needs to consider alternatives, and that sometimes takes patience and vocabulary expansion. If you think you may want to author a book and haven't a clue how to begin the process, feel free to contact either author for a step-by-step approach toward writing and publishing.

One of the best ways to enhance your verbal skills, especially presentation skills, is to attend a program such as the Dale Carnegie Course. No, we don't receive a commission for referring people to this program. We do believe, however, that this and other presentation skills workshops can provide an excellent practice medium to get past shyness and a sense of inadequacy in giving presentations. Courses such as this provide a foundation of platform techniques first, followed by an opportunity to plan, give, and receive feedback for mini-presentations on a regular basis. The key to skill building is practice, and a course such as Dale Carnegie can afford a safe environment for honing one's skills.

If you have a car and a CD or DVD player in your car, then you have an opportunity to develop your verbal ability! Instead of listening to the same music over and over, why not occasionally listen to a book on tape? Not only will you be entertained, but you will be hearing words that are new (or words you know used in different ways). Of course you could also listen to audiotapes of workshops and conferences with the same end result.

Our final recommendation for expanding verbal ability is to volunteer to act in a local theater group. Not each of us is a "ham" that wants to take center stage; however, many local theater groups need people who are willing to audition for smaller parts. Acting can take us outside of ourselves and serve as a wonderful stress reducer, and can provide a way to become less intimidated by an audience. (By the way, with the stage lights it's impossible to tell whether there's an audience of 10 or 100!)

Linda recently was asked to participate in a short video segment in an orientation video for an online course she's teaching. She had to develop and write a five-minute script to cover key points succinctly and professionally. What a great challenge! If you have opportunities like this presented to you, we encourage you to accept and learn from them.

## Enhancing Your Logic and Analysis Abilities

We've often heard people say, "I can't make good decisions," or, "I get mired down in the details." If you find yourself among this group, we have some suggestions to help you improve your analysis and objective decision-making skills.

There are some excellent seminars at local universities on Decision Making. Linda teaches one at Xavier University that covers steps in objective decision making, identifying the true problem, generating sound alternatives, and analyzing the results of a decision. In order to enhance analysis skills, it's necessary to first have a framework for effective decision making. We recommend that you investigate workshops of this nature in your area.

Whenever you're faced with a personal or workplace dilemma, do you make a pro's/con's list of potential solutions? This is a technique called Force Field Analysis, using the framework below (table 10.1).

Let's insert an example to demonstrate how you would use this tool. When Linda was trying to decide whether she should quit her full-time position as Court Administrator for a U.S. Court of Appeals and pursue a Ph.D., these were her considerations (table 10.2).

Force field analysis helped Linda to think through factors that would enable her to quit her position and return to school and to be realistic about areas in her life that would be affected negatively. The positive factors outweighed the negatives (although this isn't always the case). Even if the negative factors are higher, that simply means that consideration must be given to how these factors can be minimized. For instance, a significant negative factor for Linda was the necessity to earn some income during her

**Table 10.1**   Force Field Analysis

Potential Solution:_____

| + | − |
|---|---|
| Factors that support solution | Factors that hinder solution |
| Impact | Impact |
| 1 to 3 | 1 to 3 |
| 1 to 3 | 1 to 3 |
| 1 to 3 | 1 to 3 |
| Total | Total |

**Table 10.2**   Example of Force Field Analysis

Potential Solution to Career Restlessness: Quit Job and Pursue a Ph.D.

| Factors that support solution | | Factors that hinder solution | |
|---|---|---|---|
| Desire for ongoing education | 3 | Would need to work part time | 3 |
| Husband supportive of ongoing education | 2 | Starting at age 40 | 1 |
| One year of income in bank | 2 | Friends' disapproval | 1 |
| Totals | 7 | | 5 |

Impact Legend:   3 – high impact   2 – moderate impact   1 – slight impact academic detour. So she elected to start a consulting practice and pursue part-time assignments for supplemental income to her husband's salary.

Process mapping is an excellent tool to visually show the flow of work. Many process improvement teams use this method to identify work bottlenecks and duplication of effort. The exercise of process mapping could help you to hone your logic and analysis skills. You could begin with something you know well: your own job. Take one function and map each step, then look at the final results and ask yourself, "where do bottlenecks occur?" or, "where is there replication of effort?" A sample process map, Manager, Payroll and Benefits—Employee Change Input, is shown below in figure 10.1.

Not everyone is a chess or checkers aficionado; however, these games would be excellent and fun ways to improve your logical thought processes. For either game, it's necessary to project ahead several moves to consider the "what if's": if I move this piece, what might my opponent be able to do as a consequence? Chess in particular takes patience and thinking ahead several moves, so mastery of this game will help you open the pathways in your brain to logical thinking.

Our final recommendation is for you to go back to school! Well, not for a degree, but for a single class or two. You can take a small number of undergraduate or even graduate-level courses without registering for the entire program, and we suggest an undergraduate class in Statistics. Hate the idea? Look for a college or junior college that employs adjunct faculty who live "in the real world" and are teaching part-time. Instructors with this background are excellent because they provide practical applications rather than pure theory.

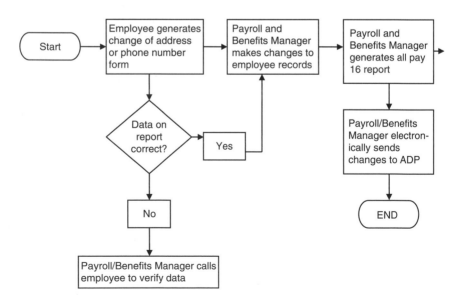

**Figure 10.1**    Manager, Payroll, and Benefits—Employee Change Input

## Enhancing Your Visual/Spatial Abilities

We've heard many of our friends and coworkers say, "I'm just not creative!" You may have more creativity locked inside you than you realize. The key to unlocking that creative bent is to engage in some different types of activities to stretch those "brain muscles."

One suggestion is to take an art or photography class, even if you haven't ever had an interest in pursuing either as an avocation, let alone a vocation. This type of class will guide you toward leaning on your visual sense of proportion and color and placing items in relationship to one another for the best possible effect. Linda, who scored abysmally in all the 8th grade standardized tests on visual/spatial ability, took a series of photography classes when she was twenty-one. She stretched her visual senses to appreciate how objects look juxtaposed to one another and to understand how to frame an excellent shot so that people and scenery are shown to their best advantage.

This may sound strange, especially for you ladies: take a basic auto repair class at a local high school or vocational school. Auto mechanics must have a solid sense of "what goes where" and the impact of one part on several other parts. This type of class will provide you with the knowledge to understand what estimates *really* mean and heighten your "feel" for shapes and sizes of objects.

A practice you can engage in while you're all alone is to write directions to your house from several different locations. This exercise promotes a sense of geography and your seeing in your "mind's eye" where the target location is in relationship to a fixed point. As you become more adept at this skill, people to whom you provide directions will be very grateful!

You can enhance your visual/spatial skills and have fun at the same time by purchasing and playing with children's building block toys, such as LEGO. While some of the toys are fairly basic, LEGO also has more sophisticated toys to put together, such as race cars and rocket ships, which are definitely challenging. If you have young children or grandchildren, you're in luck—you can use them as your "cover" to practice!

Another suggestion is along the same lines as LEGO, and that's putting airplanes together from a kit. As with other kits, these can run from basic to quite complicated and intricate, with hundreds of tiny parts. Putting these airplanes together requires transference of the visual on paper (the instructions) to an actual object in your hand. An added bonus is that this process will help build your patience and persistence.

## Enhancing Intrapersonal Skills

More men than women have confessed to us that this is a weak area for them because they weren't encouraged as children to be introspective and reflective. Yet, one of the best ways to minimize making the same mistake twice is to reflect on lessons learned from past errors in judgment. The suggestions below are intended to get you more in tune with yourself and build your understanding of why you do the things you do.

Our first recommendation is the one that we made earlier: for you to start a journal and keep it up on a daily basis. You may be thinking, "what do I write about?" Write about what you did that day, your dreams and how you moved forward to achieving those dreams, and the people with whom you interacted and how they affected you. Those we know who keep a journal have reported this to be very cathartic because they can vent their feelings without actually saying something out loud that they'll regret later. Going back over what you've written in the previous month can provide insights to how certain people, events, and the world around you affect and influence your behaviors.

If you haven't had an opportunity to take a personality profile such as the Myers-Briggs Type Indicator (MBTI) or True Colors, this could provide insights into your personality and why you react the way you do to certain people or situations. These indicators are not "tests"—they can't be failed. Through a series of event-centered or people-centered questions, these profiles assess the way people accept information, process that information, and respond to the world around them. When Linda took the MBTI years ago, she had that "aha" moment that comes to those who aren't sure why some people just push all their buttons, or why some situations are clearly uncomfortable.

A career coach could also help you understand your true wants and desires; specifically, in terms of the direction you want to take your career. If you're solid on that front, you might consider a life coach whose role is to ask you the tough questions: What do you really want out of life? What makes you happy? What volunteer activities will help you grow personally and professionally? The coach does not answer the questions for you. The coach guides you toward finding the answers and being truthful with yourself first and foremost.

## Enhancing Interpersonal Skills

Have you ever been to a business reception in which a person attached herself to you and didn't get the message when you tried to politely extricate yourself from the conversation in order to move on and continue mingling? Perhaps you dropped the hint that you needed to refresh your drink and catch up with a colleague, and she moved right along to the bar with you, talking all the while. This is a person who doesn't have balanced interpersonal skills—she can talk just fine; it's knowing when to end the conversation that's a problem.

In this section, we'll offer concrete suggestions to enhance the all-important interpersonal dimension of EQ, which includes components such as empathy, social responsibility, and professional relationships.

Our first recommendation is to take a course on negotiation or conflict resolution. Courses of this type focus on ways to consider others' needs and wants in order to problem solve effectively. Successful conflict resolution requires that all parties involved think creatively to find ways to improve a process or address a problem. Conflict resolution workshops teach people to "get over themselves" and think about what others might want in order to agree to a course of action. These workshops also teach people to articulate their own wants and needs effectively so their feelings are clearly understood.

Let's go back to the Dale Carnegie courses for a moment. In these workshops, people are required to write and present speeches on assigned topics. Participants must conduct the research, write their remarks, and present in front of a "friendly" audience of their peers. This is a safe environment in that everyone else is in the same position going in—fearful of making public presentations.

Most fields have a professional organization that meets on a regular basis, such as the Society for Human Resource Management. Membership and active involvement on a committee are wonderful ways to enhance interpersonal skills. To best take advantage of membership, go to most of the meeting during the social hour and walk from group to group to introduce yourself. Join a committee so that you know at least those people in the organization. Linda joined her local SHRM chapter early in her career and immediately signed on for the Membership Committee. In that capacity, she volunteered to meet potential or new members at the door and take them around and introduce them. This forced her to meet and talk with the membership herself, and she later became a local chapter President!

Another step that Linda took early on in her life in order to eliminate some of her shyness and improve her interpersonal skills was to get involved in acting, first in high school and then in community theater. In order to take on another person's persona, it's necessary to think beyond yourself and consider what another person is thinking or needing. This is what interpersonal skills are about, really: understanding what others want and need and responding to that knowledge appropriately. Linda has had an opportunity to play a wide range of characters, from an Irish school girl to a legal secretary to a cheating wife. To do this with any level of credibility, it's necessary to empathize with the character, and empathy is a key element of interpersonal skills.

If you don't tune in to peoples' "body language" during conversations, start doing this. If there's a discrepancy between the words someone is saying and their body language, discount the words and rely on the message they're sending inadvertently. Having a sense of the entire message helps you become a better listener, ask probe questions when there is a disconnect between body language and words, and takes you "out of yourself" to build better interpersonal skills.

A way to enhance your concept of social responsibility is to become involved in civic meetings, such as town hall meetings or council meetings.

You can be somewhat passive in that you simply sit in the audience and observe the discussions about community events. This would at least provide the opportunity to stay current on events going on around you that affect your neighborhood. If you really want to go a step further, you could volunteer to participate as a fund raiser or to take surveys. The more you learn, the more you'll understand that your actions, such as recycling, have an impact on people outside the walls of your home.

Our last suggestion serves many purposes: get a dog, take it for walks, and talk to other walkers. If you're not comfortable just starting a conversation with people you meet, a dog is a terrific vehicle to break down barriers. Linda is 5 feet 2 inches tall and she had an Irish Wolfhound (about 100 pounds) for several years. She couldn't walk more than a block without someone stopping to comment about that!

Our central message in this chapter is a simple one: you can build dimensions of your EI on a day by day basis. We've offered a few suggestions in order to get you thinking, and we're certain you can use them as a springboard for even more techniques!

# CHAPTER ELEVEN

# Here's Your Checklist for Application!

In this chapter, we'll summarize key points from the book in a checklist format that emphasizes areas that will help you support your organization's strategic business imperatives.

Emotional Intelligence in the Needs Analysis Process (from chapter 3):

- Have you ascertained how objectives in upcoming educational or training events support your company's mission? vision? key business imperatives?
- Have you identified a pattern across management staff in terms of gaps in core competencies? If so, do you have an action plan to add these gaps into the educational curriculum?
- Has your management staff identified a pattern across employees in terms of gaps in core competencies? If so, do you have an action plan to add these gaps into the educational curriculum?
- Are there specific areas in your organization in which productivity and quality are often low? Have you identified whether the cause is skills related, or something else?
- Do employees have the resources required to apply skills and knowledge acquired in recent training activities?

Emotional Intelligence in Training and Educational Design (from chapter 4). As a trainer or leader, have you:

- Defined the target audience? Knowing something about your audience will help you not only on day one but also in the long run.
- Selected audience appropriate activities? (Androgogical versus Pedagogical).
- Sequenced your objectives accordingly?
- Considered both methods and materials geared toward your audiences' learning preferences?
- Allowed for flexibility and are willing and able to revise if necessary?

When choosing the Right Trainer or Consultant do you:

- Require trainers/consultants to provide an outline in advance of each scheduled training event?
- Observe trainers/consultants when they're presenting on the topic for which you're considering them?
- Discuss with potential trainers/consultants how they plan to measure the success of their training endeavors?

It's Show Time: The Emotionally Intelligent Trainer in Action (from chapter 5).
    As a trainer or teacher, do you:

- Stay in the moment during training so you can be sensitive and respond to participants' questions and concerns?
- Ask questions frequently during training in order to draw in participants?
- Listen to the answers to the questions you ask during training?
- Tune in to participants' "body language"?
- Provide a reading list for participants in advance of training events?

Emotional Intelligence and the Measurement Process (from chapter 6).
    Does your organization:

- Establish written objectives for each educational event?
- Evaluate all training events on the reaction, learning, behavior, results and ROI levels?
- Provide trainees with an action plan at the end of training events and work with them to ensure it succeeds?
- Discontinue training activities that don't clearly demonstrate added value?

How to Develop Your EQ as a Trainer or Leader (from chapter 7).

- Believe!
- Accept that you won't please everyone and do your best to please the majority.
- Gain "buy in" early on (from the top down).
- Ensure everyone is on the "same page."
- Anticipate and prepare for obstacles.
- Have a Plan B (and "C" and "D," and so on, if necessary).
- Communicate—answer the 5 Ws and the 1 H (Who, What, Where, When, Why, and How).
- Practice!
- Learn from Mistakes.

# CHAPTER TWELVE

# A Self-Assessment on Emotional Intelligence

## Overview of Instrument

After completing the research for this book, we decided to synthesize what we had learned about Emotional Intelligence (EI) into an assessment that is straightforward and easy to take. Our objective was to develop a self-assessment instrument that addresses five areas of EI: verbal agility, logic and quantitative skills, visual–spatial ability, self-awareness (intrapersonal skills), and interpersonal skills. A copy of the instrument is included as Appendix 18. We administered this self-assessment to fifty of our surveyed trainers and found a correlation between a high EI and effective training. By "effective," we are referring to concrete measures such as increased productivity, fewer customer complaints, increased profitability, and less management time required to handle employee issues and problems.

Our surveyed trainers scored an average of 18 in verbal agility, 17 in visual–spatial ability, 22 in logic and quantitative skills, 29 in self-awareness, and 28 in interpersonal skills. Although we intend to continue using the self-assessment in ongoing work in the area of training and EI, we believe this initial finding to be very promising in support of our assertion that successful trainers have a high degree of EI.

## Taking and Scoring the Self-Assessment

The assessment contains twenty-five one-sentence items. Each item is designed to capture a single element of EI. As you read through the items, place the response you believe most accurately reflects how you are today to the left of each item. A Likert-type scale rates your responses from 1 to 5—a rating of 5 being almost always rare. The assessment should take between 5 and 10 minutes to complete and score.

Four of the items relate to verbal agility: #1, #8, #9, and #14. A low score (4 to 8) on this area of EI indicates only that you may not currently possess a large vocabulary or know when to use specific words or phrases for different audiences. For instance, you may have a large technical vocabulary because of the job you hold. If you're making a presentation to people outside your technical area of expertise, you would want to craft the discussion in a way that would minimize the use of technical jargon. Perhaps because you have a limited vocabulary, you may shy away from facilitating team meetings or speaking in front of even small groups. Not to worry. EI in this, and the other four areas, can be developed with effort and time (refer back to chapter 10!).

If you scored high (17 to 20) in the verbal agility area, you are very likely in an occupation or avocation that allows you to play with words, and write articles or even books. You probably challenge yourself to learn new words or phrases on a regular basis. You can easily leverage this competency into writing training materials, facilitating corporate training, or leading team meetings.

Five of the items relate to quantitative analysis and logic: #2, #3, #10, #15, and #17. A low score (5 to 10) in this competency may mean that you get bored with theoretical, scientific explanations or are not facile with quantitative analysis. You probably steer away from doing your own taxes! On the other hand, if you scored high (21 to 25) in this area, you seek out your own logical explanations to why events occur, rather than accept at face value others' version of events. You probably tend to take a linear approach toward solving problems and dig deeply into issues before making a decision. This competency is critical for conducting training needs assessments and tailoring training events to address skills gaps uncovered during the process.

Four of the items relate to visual-spatial ability: #4, #11, #16, and #21. A low score (4 to 8) indicates that you have difficulty forming clear mental pictures when someone is trying to explain how something works. You may find reading and following maps to be a challenge, as well as following verbal directions. If you have a high score (17 to 20), you like to engage in experiential learning and pick up new concepts quite easily through this learning method. You probably solve puzzles easily! As a trainer or leader, this competency will help you to grasp why a participant is having difficulty understanding a concept or approach, even though he or she may provide only sketchy feedback about why they're having difficulty with the material.

Six of the items relate to self-awareness or intrapersonal skills: #5, #6, #12, #19, #22, and #24. If you have a low score (6 to 12) in this competency, you are probably challenged with decisions such as which job to take or which option to choose among several training activities. You may be fuzzy about the reason you've held beliefs over the years, such as a belief about what colors look best on you. If your score is high in this area (25 to 30), you take ownership for you beliefs and actions and have a high level of confidence in your decisions. You're tuned in to what assignments are best for you and where you have shortcomings. You're not likely to take on a training project in a field where you have little or no experience or expertise!

There are also six items that relate to interpersonal skills: #7, #13, #18, #20, #23, and #25. A low score (6 to 12) indicates that you don't pick up others' moods easily or understand others' feelings that to someone else might be quite obvious. If you scored high (25 to 30) in this area, you can often pick up others' mood through watching their "body language" or listening to their tone of voice. You're likely energized by people and are comfortable in large groups, whether as a speaker or group member. A trainer who has a high level of competency in this area has overcome a huge hurdle that most people have: fear of public speaking!

### How to Use the Self-Assessment to Select Trainers

Picture in your mind a person that you believe to be an excellent trainer (maybe it's you!). Consider the attributes this person possesses that lead you to conclude that he or she is effective. When we think about great trainers we've known over the years, descriptors like "energetic," "curious," "caring," "good listener," and "critical thinking skills" come immediately to mind.

A person's self-assessment will definitely be skewed somewhat (depending on how high on the self-awareness scale they are), so we recommend this tool as *one* of several methods you use to select trainers. People who are aware of their strengths and skills gaps—and have the willingness to take steps to minimize the gaps—surfaced in our surveys as the most effective trainers. We suggest that this instrument can complement observation, feedback from participants, and interviews in the trainer selection process.

# CHAPTER THIRTEEN

# *Now What? The Path Forward*

Perhaps by now you've elected to take the self-assessment provided in Appendix 18. You may or may not be satisfied with the score you received. If you want to enhance your leadership and training EQ, you can. We have provided some suggestions for concrete EQ developmental activities in chapter 10, and we hope you'll try some of them out.

We suggest you start with "My EI Development Plan," shown below. Following this template, there are additional suggestions about how to complete a development plan.

## My EI Development Plan

Directions: Evaluate your EI results and decide on a high priority goal. You can focus on leveraging an EI strength or enhancing a weaker area.

My EI goal is to:

If I achieve this goal, what's the best that could happen?

- 
- 

If I do not achieve this goal, what's the worst that could happen?

- 
- 

Development Activities           Target Completion Date

1.
2.
3.

Barriers to achieving this goal are:        Strategies to minimize barrier:

How will I know that I'm achieving this goal?

Measures:

One of the dimensions of EI is our ability to understand ourselves. That is, are we realistic about our strengths and weaknesses, talents, and skill sets? We encourage you to use this book as a stepping off point toward achieving the next level of skills you'll need as a leader and trainer or educator. Here are some suggestions for how to use this development guide.

## My EI Goal

Is there an area of professional and personal development you believe (or your boss believes) is necessary in order for you to move forward in your career or in your social life? At work, perhaps you've been told more than once that your instructions aren't clear, for instance. This is a widespread barrier across many organizations, and it gets in the way of productivity and customer satisfaction. Perhaps you'd like to be more of an empathetic listener than you are today so you fully understand other peoples' perspectives, not only at work but at home too. Whatever your goal is, write it down. Remember the acronym S-M-A-R-T as you're writing your goals; that is, they are specific, measurable, achievable, realistic, and time sensitive.

## If I Achieve This Goal

If you achieve the goal you wrote down above, what will happen? How will the improvement enhance your personal or professional life? Will your relationships with coworkers or direct reports be improved? Will your ability to design and deliver training programs be enhanced?

## If I Do Not Achieve This Goal

What are the consequences if your EI does not change in any way and you don't achieve the desired goal? Will you be embarrassed because you receive poor feedback on training evaluations? Will you be less likely to sell your ideas to upper management? Will you lose valuable employees that report to you? What's the driver that will motivate you to work toward building your EI score?

## Development Activities

We've provided some ideas in chapter 10. Here are some additional tasks and assignments that you could take on to develop specific competencies:

Competency:   Communication Skills.
Assignments:   Develop a Communications Plan to Advise Employees of a Change in Product, Procedures, or Processes.
Facilitate Employee Meetings to Solicit Process Improvement Ideas.
Develop and Deliver a Training Session on the Company's Core Values.
Write a Column in the In-House Newsletter or an Industry Newsletter.
Develop and Deliver Industry Presentations.
Shadow in the Customer Service and Public Relations Departments for a Week.
Work with Higher Manager who is Particularly Good at Communication.
Reading List:   *Getting To Yes*, Fisher and Ury.
   *Influence Without Authority*, Cohen and Bradford.
Course(s):   Conflict Resolution.

Competency:   Customer Orientation.
Assignments:   Facilitate a Monthly Roundtable with Customers.
Establish a S.I.P.O.C. Process Flow Chart (Suppliers-Inputs-Process-Outputs-Customers) for All Key Activities in Division.
Establish and Lead or Champion a Cross Functional Process Improvement Team.
Develop and Distribute a "Customer" Survey; Develop an Action Plan Based on the Results.
Develop an Organizational Code of Ethics.
Reading List:   *Service America!*, Albrecht and Zemke.
Course(s):   Customer Service—The Disney Way.
   The Guest: Everything You Already Know about Customer Service.
   Give 'em The Pickle.

Competency:   Innovation and Entrepreneurship.
Assignments:   Shadow the Team that Conceptualizes and Designs New Products.
Serve on New Project/Product Review Committee.
Responsibility to Start Up a New Company or Division.
Assess the Last Group of Incoming Customer Surveys to Generate Ideas for New Approaches or Products.

Summarize New Trends/Techniques: Present to Others.
Facilitate Strategic Planning of Another Division or Business Unit
Interview Vendors and Suppliers about their Trends and Issues; Develop a Collaborative Approach toward Addressing Those Trends for Competitive Advantage.
Assignment of "undoable" Project (the last person who tried it failed).

| | |
|---|---|
| Reading List: | Historical Articles about the Industry. |
| | Biographies on Leaders in the Industry. |
| Course(s): | Decision Making. |
| | Creativity. |

Competency:      Managing Workplace Diversity.

Assignments:    Develop and Deliver a Workshop on Cultural Diversity (or any diversity topic).
Take an Overseas Assignment or Assignment in Another State.
Learn Another Language Specific to Your Work, Such as Spanish for Production Workers on Audiotape—Teach to One or More Colleagues.
Collaborate with Human Resources to Develop a Diversity Initiative.

| | |
|---|---|
| Reading List: | *Beyond Race and Gender,* Thomas. |
| | *The Diversity Machine,* Lynch. |
| | *Bridging the Generation Gap,* Gravett and Throckmorton. |
| Course(s): | Society for Human Resource Management |
| | Diversity Conferences (National and Local Chapters). |

Competency:      Managing Change

Assignments:    Develop and Implement a Communications Plan to Advise about a Change in Product, Procedures, or Processes.
Assess Incoming Customer Surveys to Ascertain Why They Buy (a) From our Company and (b) From Competitors.
Facilitate Roundtables with Each Business Unit and Help Identify Their Competitive Differentiators.
Develop a Contingency Plan If a Key Supplier Went Out of Business.

| | |
|---|---|
| Reading List: | Subscriptions: |
| | Fast Company. |
| | Wall Street Journal. |
| | Harvard Business Review. |
| | Books: |
| | *Riding the Waves of Change,* Morgan. *Who Moved My Cheese,* Johnson and Blanchard. |
| Course(s): | Change Management. |

Competency:     Mastery of Technology.
Assignments:    Shadow Staff in the M.I.S. Department.
                Take One Workshop Each Quarter on a New Company
                Technology.
                Attend M.I.S. Department Staff Meetings for Six Months.
                Create a Symbol/Rallying Cry for Change and
                Implementation.
                Supervise Liquidation of Product, Program, Equipment,
                or System.
                Manage Ad Hoc Group in a Rapidly Expanding
                Operation.
                Reading List:   Subscriptions:
                                E-Executive.
                                TW—Trend Watch.
                                P—Producer.
                                CIO Magazine and www.cio.com
                                CSO Magazine and www.csoonline.com
                                Computerworld and www.computer-
                                world.com
                Course(s):      Elluminate.
                                Blackboard.
                                Distance Learning.
Competency:     Objective Setting and Results Orientation to Achieve
                Strategic Plans.
Assignments:    Benchmark and Analyze Strategic Planning Methods
                of 3–5 Global Organizations: Present Results to
                Colleagues.
                Facilitate the Strategic Planning Session of Another
                Division within the Organization.
                Identify the Processes and Activities that
                ProvideCompetitors with an Advantage: Present Results
                to Colleagues.
                Coach Director-Level and Mid Manager-Level Staff Through
                Their Strategic Planning Sessions.
                Develop a Written Action Plan to Share Learnings from
                Organizational Failures to Managers and Directors.
                Join a Task Force to Develop a Performance Management
                Process that Supports Strategic Plan Execution.
                Champion a Continuous Improvement Recommendation
                or a Process Improvement Team.
                Do a Problem Prevention Analysis.
                Design New, Simpler Effectiveness Measures.
                Reading List:   *The Balanced Scorecard*, Kaplan and Norton.
                                *First, Break All the Rules*, Buckingham
                                and Kaufman.
                                *Creating a Culture of Competence*, Zwell.

Course(s):    SMART Goal Setting.
              High Powered Strategies for Innovative
              Problem-Solving and Decision Making.

Competency:   Team Work

Assignments:  Manage Ad Hoc Group of Inexperienced People.
              Create a Rewards and Recognition System that Reinforces Interdependent, Joint Goals.
              Establish an Internal/External Team with Clients/Vendors to Shorten Cycle Times, Reduce Bottlenecks, or Improve Responsiveness to Customers.
              Champion a Process Improvement Team.
              Deal with a Business Crisis.
              Facilitate a Roundtable with Other Business Units to Identify Their Competitive Differentiators.
              Lead an Off-Site Executive Team Retreat to Identify and Leverage the Synergism Across Units.

Reading List: *How to Make Collaboration Work: Powerful Ways to Build Consensus, Solve Problems, and Make Decisions*, Straus and Layton.
              *The Collaborative Leadership Fieldbook*, Chrislip.
              *The Collaboration Challenge*, Austin;
              *The Carrot Principle*, Gostick and Elton.

Course(s):    The Dysfunctions of a Team, Best Coaching, Mentoring and Teambuilding Skills.

## Barriers to Achieving This Goal

Speaking of being realistic, this is the time to use the "force field analysis" approach and reflect on potential barriers that push against your chances for successfully achieving your EQ goal. Perhaps you're working full-time and going to school part-time. Time issues are sure to be a problem for additional personal development. So you'll need to consider some strategies to minimize that barrier, such as asking a friend or relative to babysit occasionally or hiring a cleaning service so you have time for yourself. Prioritizing will also be a key with time issues. If it's important to you, you will find time or a way to make it happen. Or, practice saying "no" when it's necessary! Explain your goal and that will not only help keep you accountable, but people will understand and maybe even encourage you and offer assistance before you have to ask. Give it a try.

The second part of this section, Target Completion Dates, is important too! Our research over the years has found that people respond best to stretch goals that have a finite time frame for achievement. Be realistic considering your time constraints; however, be sure to write down target dates for each activity.

## How Will I Know I'm Achieving This Goal?

If you don't know where you're going, any destination will do! This section is intended to provide a framework for success. What's happening in your life now that you don't like—the reason for setting the EQ goal that you did? When that issue is no longer a concern, you will know you're achieving your goal. A tangible measure for trainers is, of course, evaluations turned in at the end of training. If workshop participants used to write that you don't allow enough time for group interaction or don't listen to questions—and the comments stop after you begin working on this behavior—you'll know that you're achieving your goal. If your goal is to manage the stress of giving performance evaluations and your development plan is to prepare more effectively, you'll know after your next performance review or two whether you're meeting your goal.

Developing one's Emotional Intelligence is an ongoing process, a lifelong process. We encourage you to make the long term commitment to take even small steps on a regular basis to enhance your ability to relate to the world around you. The results will be worth the effort!

*Appendices*

# Appendix 1

## Survey Compilation: Trainers

N = 50

1. When conducting a training session, for the initial greeting, I'm most likely to:
   (a) Stand at the door and greet participants as they enter (7)
   (b) Acknowledge people individually after they are seated (37)
   (c) Wait to address the entire group together (6)
   (d) Skip the greeting and get to business (0)

Key Themes from Comments:
   - Participants might feel like the "salesperson is coming" if approached at the door
   - A smile or a wave as people enter is sufficient
   - Consider having staff and a registration table outside the meeting room

2. If participants are entering the training room and I'm still preparing flip charts, I am most likely to:
   (a) Glance up and smile but continue writing my flip charts (11)
   (b) Verbally welcome participants and direct them to refreshments and/or to their seats (29)
   (c) Stop writing on the clip charts and mingle with participants (10)
   (d) Focus completely on finishing the flip charts rather than acknowledge individuals as they enter the classroom (0)

Key Themes from Comments:
   - The tone needs to be welcoming and say "I'm glad you're here"
   - Take the opportunity to build rapport with participants early in the process
   - Do as much preprep as feasible so that you appear ready, yet can talk with participants at the beginning

3. I think ice breakers are:
   (a) Very useful and always good (7)
   (b) Semi-useful and used frequently in my training sessions (12)
   (c) Dependent on the subject matter as to whether or not they're utilized (28)
   (d) A waste of time (3)

Key Themes from Comments:
   - Before they're used, consider the audience and the topic for appropriateness
   - Tailor ice breakers to the level of participants
   - Ice breakers might be threatening to some individuals or groups

4. If I'm sharing some information with the class and two people are holding a distracting side conversation, I will probably:
   (a) Talk louder (2)
   (b) Ignore them (6)
   (c) Keep talking, but walk over to stand near the area where the sidebar is being held (38)
   (d) Stop and ask the people who are talking to be quiet (4)

Key Themes from Comments:
   • The facilitator must handle distractions but in a way that doesn't "turn the crowd" against him or her
   • Set a tone that mutual respect is a ground rule, right from the beginning

5. When a training class participant challenges a point I've made, I'm most likely to:
   (a) Tell the person he/she is wrong (3)
   (b) Defer to the other person's opinion (2)
   (c) Ask for other participants to validate my point (8)
   (d) Ask the person to express his or her perspective (37)

Key Themes from Comments:
   • If facts are in dispute, point to the facts and gently advise participant of his/her misunderstanding
   • Asking for input from others promotes peer influence, which can be powerful
   • A quality facilitator promotes discussion and respectful disagreement

6. When I don't know the answer:
   (a) I make up something and pretend I know (0)
   (b) Ask for someone else to respond (26)
   (c) Admit I don't know (9)
   (d) Tell the participants I'll find out the answer and get back to them (15)

Key Themes from Comments:
   • A strong facilitator promotes sharing and doesn't always have to be the answer-giver
   • People will know if you try to fake it, sooner or later, then you'll lose credibility

7. If the class appears to be bored during the middle of a training session, I usually:
   (a) Stay on my agenda and hope things improve (0)
   (b) Take five minutes out and tell some jokes (8)
   (c) Break participants into discussion groups with a pertinent case study (38)
   (d) Ask participants what they'd rather do (4)

Key Themes from Comments:
   • "Wishin and hopin" doesn't improve any situation—be proactive
   • If it's been a long day, some humor may help, but don't let the session get away from you
   • A case study or activity that's "real" should help people reenergize
   • If you ask participants what they want to do, they may just leave

8. During a whole-group discussion about a seemingly benign topic, a workshop participant bursts into tears. You are most likely to:
   (a) Call a ten-minute break so the person can calm down (12)
   (b) Ignore the situation (2)
   (c) Call a short break and talk to the person to see if you can assist (24)
   (d) Tell the person he/she may be excused to pull him/herself together (12)

Key Themes from Comments:
   - You don't need to diagnose the problem, but you should demonstrate that you care about the individual (see what's going on so you can decide the next step)
   - This situation would distract others if it's ignored

9. When a session runs longer or shorter than planned, I will:
   (a) Ensure the agenda is completed regardless of time (4)
   (b) Add "fluff" to fill time or cut out irrelevant information to shorten the session (19)
   (c) Finish on time but assign "homework" whether it be in class or at home (22)
   (d) Move to the next subject even if it's a day early or late (5)

Key themes from Comments:
   - Participants are mentally gone after the publicized stop time; don't try to go on
   - It's important to cover mutually agreed on material; do process checks periodically to discover what those points are
   - Agendas are like some rules—meant to be broken

10. If something goes wrong, such as the room not being set up or the time is changed or the training materials are missing, I normally will:
   (a) Ad lib (8)
   (b) Cancel the session (5)
   (c) Postpone and re-schedule the session (8)
   (d) Move to "Plan B" and do a different activity (29)

Key Themes from Comments:
   - Flexibility is critical; go in with contingency plans
   - A session is better rescheduled than be of poor quality

11. As a trainer, my thoughts on continuous learning to shore up my knowledge base are:
   (a) I'm the trainer, so I'm already the expert and don't need to learn more (0)
   (b) I'm always open to learning more (12)
   (c) I'm careful with who/where I accept information (35)
   (d) It's nice to know, yet it's not practical for me to continually update my training materials (3)

Key Themes from Comments:
   - Take a planned, strategic approach to ongoing learning—be current on key issues that affect your organization and its success
   - Be selective about resources; stay at the cutting edge

12. With respect to revising training materials, I try to tweak my training programs:
    (a) Every time I use them (20)
    (b) Once every year (18)
    (c) Only when I'm told (0)
    (d) Rarely, if ever (12)

Key Themes from Comments:
   • Updating materials keeps me current and fresh in my thinking
   • Practically speaking, if you do frequent training, you can't update every time
   • Keep abreast of changes and include changes such as new laws or regs

13. What process do you use to prepare for a training session whether you have or haven't worked with the group before?
    (a) I meet with the training coordinator (15)
    (b) I meet with some of the actual participants (26)
    (c) I meet with the supervisor of the attendees (9)
    (d) I don't meet with anyone in advance (0)

Key Themes from Comments:
   • The participants' supervisors aren't always aware of their direct reports' needs
   • A profile of participants in advance helps me prepare better

14. To measure the results of your training, what method do you use the most?
    (a) A survey as soon as the session is complete to assess their feelings about the content, the setting, and myself (4)
    (b) A test to ensure they understand the material just presented (4)
    (c) Observation to see firsthand their newly acquired behavior in action (9)
    (d) Actual data such as volume, profitability, or quantity (33)

Key Themes from Comments:
   • Training must first and foremost be aligned with strategic objectives: that's the success criteria
   • The ROI. approach to training is significant and lends credibility to training activities

15. Who has been the biggest obstacle you've had to overcome with respect to gaining "buy in"?
    (a) Top management, executives, CEO/President level leadership (7)
    (b) Direct supervisors or line managers (28)
    (c) Coworkers of those being trained (9)
    (d) Participants themselves (6)

Key Themes from Comments:
   • Frontline supervisors have a significant impact on whether trainees employ tools and techniques learned
   • There's some trickle-down effect from top levels if training is truly supported
   • If participants help set training objectives, they buy in much quicker

# *Appendix 2*

## Pre-Workshop Audience Analysis

Date of Presentation:_____ Topic:_____

Purpose of Presentation:_____

Key Points and Priorities:_____

_____

Time Allotted:_____

Presenter(s):_____  _____

_____  _____

Audience Participants:

Name      Title/Function      Organization      Issues, Concerns, Expectations

_____

_____

_____

_____

_____

_____

_____

_____

Proprietary Information/Competitor Sensitive Information:_____

_____

_____

Desired Action(s) Following Presentation:_____

Participant Organization Profile:

Mission Statement:_____

_____

Key Financial Statistics:_____

Decision Makers:

Name:_____

Title:_____

Core Products and Services:_____

_____

Primary Competitors:_____

_____

# *Appendix 3*

## Sample: Setting Time Frames for
## a 30–Minute Presentation

| IDEA # | Priority: 1 to 10 | Percentage | Time Allotted |
|---|---|---|---|
| 1   History of Topic | 4 | **17** $\times$ 30 (4 $\div$ 23 = 17) | 5 minutes |
| 2   Current Research | 6 | **26** $\times$ 30 | 8 minutes |
| 3   Conclusions of Research | 8 | **35** $\times$ 30 | 11 minutes |
| 4   Introduction | 2 | **9** $\times$ 30 | 2.5 minutes |
| 5   Summary | 3 | **13** $\times$ 30 | 3.5 minutes |
|  | 23 | 100% | 30 minutes |

# Appendix 4

## Organizational Culture Needs Assessment

The purpose of this survey is to provide awareness of how you and other employees feel about being a part of this organization, in order to gain insight into how we can enhance relationships and overall effectiveness. You need not include your name and phone number unless you wish to do so. Your candid answers are appreciated, and every comment will be carefully considered. Feel free to use the back of the survey or to attach additional sheets if you need more space for any questions. Please return your survey in the enclosed envelope to Dr. Linda Gravett.

1. Are you    ___Hispanic
              ___African
              ___African American
              ___Asian or Pacific Islander
              ___Caucasian
              ___American Indian or Alaskan Native
              ___East Indian

2. How long have you worked for this organization?
   ___1 year or less    ___1–2 years    ___2–3 years
   ___3–4 years    ___4–5 years    ___5–6 years
   ___6–7 years    ___7–8 years    ___9–10 years
   ___Over 10 years

3. Are you    ___Male    ___Female

4. Are you    ___Under 30    ___Under 40    ___Under 50
              ___Under 60    ___61+

5. Is your present position    ___Exempt    ___Hourly

6. What is your current level of education?
   ___High School Diploma    ___Technical/Vocational    ___Some College or GED
   ___Bachelor ___Master    ___Doctorate

7. How did you find out about the position for which you were hired into the organization?

8. How did you find out about your current position (if different from #7)?

9. Describe the type of orientation about the organization you were provided:

10. Describe the type of orientation about the department you were provided:

11. If you received on-the-job training, how would you rate the experience?
    ___Excellent        ___Good        ___Fair        ___Poor
Comments:

12(a). What other ongoing training or learning opportunities have you experienced?

12(b). How would you rate these ongoing experiences?
    ___Excellent        ___Good        ___Fair        ___Poor
Comments:

13(a). Do you feel that you fit in with other employees in your department?
    ___Yes        ___No
    Why or why not?

13(b). Do you feel that you fit in with other employees in the organization?
    ___Yes        ___No
    Why or why not?

14(a). What obstacles, if any, have you faced in feeling comfortable in this organization?

14(b). What obstacles, if any, have you faced in feeling comfortable in your department?

14(c). What obstacles, if any, have you faced in working effectively with other people in this organization?

14(d). What obstacles, if any, have you faced in working effectively with other people in your department?

15(a). Do you offer ideas and suggestions to others in your department?
    ___Yes        ___No

15(b). Do you believe that others in your department listen to your ideas and opinions?
    ___Yes        ___No
    If no, why do you think this is the case?

16(a). Do you offer ideas and suggestions to others within the organization?
    ___Yes        ___No

16(b). Do you believe that others in this organization listen to your ideas and opinions?

___Yes        ___No

If no, why do you think this is the case?

17(a). Are special assignments (e.g., task forces and committees) given within the organization based on who can best do the job?

___Yes        ___No

Please comment.

17(b). Are special assignments (e.g., task forces and committees) given within the department based on who can best do the job?

___Yes        ___No

Please comment.

18(a). What makes this organization effective?

18(b). What makes your department effective?

19(a). Have your expectations for fulfillment been met while you've been a part of this organization?

___Yes        ___No

If no, what are the reasons for your sense of unmet expectations?

19(b). Have your expectations for fulfillment been met while you've been a part of your department?

___Yes        ___No

If no, what are the reasons for your sense of unmet expectations?

20(a). Have you had mentors or coaches within this organization?

___Yes        ___No

If yes, how did these relationships evolve?

20(b). Have you had mentors or coaches within this department?

___Yes        ___No

If yes, how did these relationships evolve?

21(a). How many people in this organization have you mentored or coached?_____

How did these relationships evolve?

21(b). How many people in this department have you mentored or coached?_____

How did these relationships evolve?

22(a).  To be successful in this organization, are there any unwritten rules you are expected to follow?

___Yes                ___No

If yes, what are these unwritten rules?

22(b).  To be successful in this department, are there any unwritten rules you are expected to follow?

___Yes                ___No

If yes, what are these unwritten rules?

23.  Is there anything else you would like to comment on regarding enhancing relationships and overall effectiveness within your department or our organization? Use the back of this form, if necessary, or attach additional sheets.

Name:_____ Phone:_____

**(OPTIONAL)** Feel free to sign this survey if you'd like to be contacted by Dr. Linda Gravett to clarify or follow up on any of your responses

# *Appendix 5*

## Trust Audit: A Test for Organizational Ethics

|                                                                                        | *Yes* | *No* |
|----------------------------------------------------------------------------------------|-------|------|
| 1. I am proud of my company's image.                                                   |       |      |
| 2. Company communications are straightforward.                                         |       |      |
| 3. Policies on ethics and core values are clear.                                       |       |      |
| 4. Consensus is the primary decision style in my company.                              |       |      |
| 5. Continuous improvement is a way of life.                                            |       |      |
| 6. Change is usually a positive process in my company.                                 |       |      |
| 7. People in the company share their ideas.                                            |       |      |
| 8. Company policies are applied consistently.                                          |       |      |
| 9. Managers set a good example for ethical behavior.                                   |       |      |
| 10. My company is more productive and customer oriented because of its ethical behavior. |     |      |

Scoring: How many "no's" did you have?

| 0–3  | Excellent |
|------|-----------|
| 4–6  | Average   |
| 7–10 | Poor      |

If a majority of employees scored average or worse, your organization has room for improvement and would benefit from establishing, communicating, and implementing a Code of Ethics and Core Values.

# *Appendix 6*

## Multi–Rater Feedback Instrument

Name of Person Being Rated:_____

Title:_____

| No Opinion | Never | Rarely | Often | Always | Almost Always |
|:---:|:---:|:---:|:---:|:---:|:---:|
| 0 | 1 | 2 | 3 | 4 | 5 |

Competency:                **Communication Skills**

1. Encourages and fosters open communication.

2. Listens and responds thoughtfully to others' thoughts and ideas.

3. Assertively but politely presents thoughts and ideas.

4. Written communications are clear and precise.

5. Tailors the message to the audience.

Competency:                **Responsiveness**

1. Responds to requests or concerns in a timely manner.

2. 2. Provides honest and constructive feedback.

3. Uses a team approach to resolving systems issues.

4. Is approachable and receptive to others' ideas.

Competency:                **Leadership**

1. Serves as a role model for providing service to others.

2. Serves as a resource to peers.

3. Promotes calculated risk taking.

Competency:                **Vision**

1. Has a clear vision of where his/her department is going.

2. Sets goals and stays focused on those goals.

3. Leads the department in a direction that supports the organization.

4. Understands how to work within the industry.

Competency:                **Interpersonal Skills**

1. Acknowledges others when they've done a good job.

2. Tells others when staff has done a good job.

3. Treats others with respect.

4. Fosters collaboration.

Competency: **Consensus Building**

1. Fosters an atmosphere conducive to dialogue.

2. Promotes the problem-solving process.

3. Ensures inclusiveness in the decision-making process.

Competency: **Empowerment and Coaching**

1. Is both a teacher and a learner.

2. Serves as a resource for staff.

3. Acts as a mentor and guide.

4. Fosters continuous improvement.

# Appendix 7

## Self Assessment on Time Management

Please circle the number that best describes how you approach each statement.

| | *Always* | | | *Sometimes* | | | *Never* |
|---|---|---|---|---|---|---|---|
| 1. At the beginning of each day, I know what my primary tasks are. | 7 | 6 | 5 | 4 | 3 | 2 | 1 |
| 2. I am able to complete 1 to 3 primary tasks every day. | 7 | 6 | 5 | 4 | 3 | 2 | 1 |
| 3. I am able to complete 1 to 3 primary tasks daily *on time*. | 7 | 6 | 5 | 4 | 3 | 2 | 1 |
| 4. I do not put off difficult tasks. | 7 | 6 | 5 | 4 | 3 | 2 | 1 |
| 5. I use time management techniques. | 7 | 6 | 5 | 4 | 3 | 2 | 1 |
| 6. I schedule difficult tasks at my peak time of day. | 7 | 6 | 5 | 4 | 3 | 2 | 1 |
| 7. When time wasters occur, I handle them effectively. | 7 | 6 | 5 | 4 | 3 | 2 | 1 |
| 8. I'm not afraid to ask for help. | 7 | 6 | 5 | 4 | 3 | 2 | 1 |
| 9. I follow up with work I delegate to make sure it's on track. | 7 | 6 | 5 | 4 | 3 | 2 | 1 |
| 10. Overall, my daily tasks support my objectives and goals. | 7 | 6 | 5 | 4 | 3 | 2 | 1 |

*Scoring*:

70–49   You have mastered the essential time management concepts. Concentrate on areas where you're not meeting your goals.

48–28   You're a just under the wire worker. If you're able to gain more control over your time, you'll accomplish more primary tasks.

1–27    You're in a potential time bomb situation!  Think about how you can restructure your time and work habits.  If you do, you can probably accomplish twice as much quality work as you do now.

Sourced from *How to Get Control of Your Time and Your Life*, Alan Lakein, 1996, New American Library, New York.

# *Appendix 8*

## Quality Dialogue Questions for Focus Groups

1) I've always wondered why we...
2) I don't think we spend enough time...
3) I think we should focus on...
4) Our success lies in...
5) We are ahead of the curve...
6) We are missing a business opportunity by not...
7) I would like to be able to...
8) Everyone knows that _____, but no one will talk about it.
9) The elephant in our company is...
10) Our customers want...
11) People want to work here because...
12) The easiest thing we could do to increase morale is...
13) The easiest thing we could do to increase revenue is...
14) Our team could be more effective if...
15) Our group is effective because...
16) Our competitors admire us for...
17) I have the most difficult time when...
18) Our meetings would be more effective if...
19) Most groups feel comfortable here except...
20) I've noticed that...
21) What people in the community say about our organization is...
22) Most employees think that..., but are afraid to say it.
23) The orientation to the organization was...
24) My training while at this organization has been...
25) My job would be great if it weren't for...

# Appendix 9

## Sample Workshop Outline

Educational Effectiveness Workshop: Cultural Awareness and Diversity Training
Format: 3.5 Hours          Participants: Teaching Staff (In Groups of 30 Each)

I. Introduction and Overview                                        10 minutes

  A. Objectives
  (1) Understand the connection between learning and culture and learning and socio-economic status
  (2) Develop a framework for improving exam pass rate, including a diagnostic instrument for enrolling students

  B. Agenda and Logistics

Author Notes: Participants discover within the first 10 minutes what they'll learn; or, why are we here? The facilitator has the opportunity to set expectations and the tone of the workshop.

II. Kolb Learning Theory—Diversity of Learning Styles              1 hour

  A. Four Learning Styles and Impact on Student Behaviors 15 minutes
  (1) Abstract Conceptualizer
  (2) Concrete Experiencer
  (3) Active Experimenter
  (4) Reflective Observer

Author Notes: As teaching staff, participants learn that students have different approaches to learning and that teachers must tailor educational experiences to learning preferences.

  B. Application of Learning Styles to Distance Learning            15 minutes
  (1) Experience as a source of learning
  (2) The teacher's role in shaping learning styles
  (3) Tools and techniques for each style

  C. Discussion of Real-World Issues                               30 minutes
  (1) Breakout into small groups for discussion
  (2) Report out for each group

Author Notes: In deference to participant learning styles, this segment provides concrete tools and an opportunity for group interaction and sharing.

III. The Culture Connection—Diversity of Learning Styles           1 hour

  A. Group Activity and Discussion: My Worldview                   30 minutes

B. The Impact of Culture on Worldview                    30 minutes
(1) Commonalities and similarities across cultures in the United States today
(2) The Black learning experience
(3) Implications for teachers

Author Notes: Participants have an opportunity for individual reflection and reinforcement of how their worldview differs from others'.

10–minute break

IV. Socio-Economic Status—Diversity of Income and
Class Structure                                          30 minutes

A. Facilitator-led Discussion: Key Tenets of Payne's Book     10 minutes
(1) Application of tenets to distance learning
(2) Take-home assignment regarding individual application

Author Notes: This segment promotes learning from classmates and the instructor, as well as provides homework that puts material covered into action.

B. Proposed Diagnostic Instrument: Student Assessment     20 minutes
(1) Introduction to instrument developed by Dr. Gravett
(2) Facilitator-led discussion of application

Author Notes: Participants are provided with a concrete tool to apply in their unique setting.

V. Bringing It All Together: Development of Action Plan        30 minutes

A. Division into Seven Groups
(1) Supplemental support to students to offset the impact of adverse family dynamics
(2) Supplemental tutoring methods
(3) Techniques to obtain appropriate background information on students from Advocates and Enrollment Specialists
(4) Enhancing academic structure through deadlines for assignments and reporting of milestones
(5) Social skills training for students
(6) Tracking, reporting, and celebrating academic accomplishments
(7) Soliciting local church support

Author Notes: Participants are able to share their expertise and experience with one another.

VI. Summary and Closing                                       10 minutes

A. Summary of Key Points
B. Question and Answer Session
C. Evaluation

Author Notes: Closure is brought to the workshop and critical points are reinforced.

# Appendix 10

## Suggestions for Fielding Tough Audience Questions

1. Think about potential questions—and responses—in advance of the presentation.
2. If time is short, answer questions during your presentation very briefly, then move on.
3. Remind audience members to hold questions if too many interruptions occur.
4. Take a brief break and talk with "chatty" audience members about holding comments or questions; ask for their help in getting through the presentation objectives.
5. Offer to follow up with audience members via e-mail with lingering questions.
6. Do not try to bluff. If you don't know an answer, ask for assistance from other audience members or offer to follow up after you can find the answer.

# *Appendix 11*

## Answers to Body Language Quiz

1. c
2. b
3. c
4. d
5. c
6. a
7. c
8. a
9. c
10. b

# *Appendix 12*

## Checklist for Team Presentations

✓ Plan—and design—the presentation together

✓ Look like a team during the presentation; dress similarly (but not like twins)

✓ Have one consistent presentation style for the slides and materials used

✓ During practice, team members who aren't speaking should act as audience members

✓ Decide where each person will stand or sit during other team members' presentation

✓ In the beginning, let the audience know "who is talking about what"

✓ Pay attention to your team's presentation; you don't want to look like you're not interested!

✓ Do not talk to other team members during your presentation—project all your conversation to your audience

# Appendix 13

## Xavier Consulting Group Public Program Evaluation

We would appreciate your feedback on this program.
**Program Title:**

_____

**Date:**_____**Presenter:**_____
**Your Name:**_____**Organization:**_____
**E-mail:**_____

I. Please circle your response to each of the following:   **Not Very**   **Very**

   1. How effective was the training?                              1   2   3   4   5
   2. How do you rate the facilitator?                             1   2   3   4   5
   3. How do you rate the course materials?                        1   2   3   4   5
   4. How do you rate the training environment?                    1   2   3   4   5
   5. How do you rate the ease of the registration
      and billing processes?                                     1   2   3   4   5
   6. How do you rate the food and beverages
      provided?                                                  1   2   3   4   5
   7. How likely would you be to recommend
      this program?                                              1   2   3   4   5

II. What aspects of this program were especially beneficial?

III. How could we improve this program?

IV. In one phrase or sentence, please describe this seminar:

   May we quote you on your reaction to this program?   ☐ Yes   ☐ No
   May we refer future participants to you for comment?   ☐ Yes   ☐ No

V. Who approved you for this program? ☐ I did   ☐ The following person:

   Name_____Title_____Dept._____
   Phone#_____

VI. What other program topics or areas would you like to attend in order to further your own development?

# *Appendix 14*

## Sample Action Plan

This Action plan is a worksheet from a workshop titled *Decision Making for New Managers*, which Dr. Gravett conducts for Xavier University in Cincinnati, Ohio.

1. What decision(s) must be made within the next 30 days?

2. Who should make the decision and why?

3. What are my objectives (what does success look like)?

4. Who are my customers?

5. When is the deadline?

6. What are the potential barriers to success?

*Appendix 15*

## Name BINGO

 Find Someone Who...

Directions: Find someone who is described by each item found in the boxes below.

Have the person put his/her name in the box that describes him/her.

For each box a different person must be selected.

| is or once was school teacher | can say the alphabet backwards | misinterpreted someone | is certified in their field | belongs to MENSA |
|---|---|---|---|---|
| has "SJ" in their Meyers-Briggs profile | has witnessed someone yelling in the workplace | is a National ASTD member | is stressed out!! | is from another country |
| is a published author | speaks more than one language | attended Toastmasters | has seen someone cry at work | plays a musical instrument |
| has read the book, "First Break All the Rules" | has their Master's degree | works well under pressure | can say the alphabet backwards | has participated in a Dale Carnegie course |
| has attended a seminar to advance their education | is currently in school | plays golf | has gone on a long trip recently | needs a vacation |

# Appendix 16

## Sample Competency-Based Job Description

### *Job Description—Account Manager I*

Reports To:     Account Manager or Account Supervisor

### I. ACCOUNTABILITY

This position is accountable to assist in the development and maintenance of clients' strategic media plans as well as promotion coordination.

### II. JOB DUTIES

1) Learns and demonstrates familiarity with the local TV and radio buying process.
2) Estimates media costs using internal and external sources and presents to the Account Manager for approval.
3) Participates in the media development plan and revisions.
4) Assists in the development of guidelines and deadlines for buys for the Market Manager.
5) Develops post reports on a quarterly basis. Confers with Market Managers for explanations of Quarterly and Annual Post Reports.
6) Obtains and communicates information requested by clients by conferring with the Account Manager or Account Supervisor.
7) Develops competitive analyses for presentation to clients.
8) Assists Media Accounting in the preparation and mailing of monthly client invoices; conducts monthly invoice reconciliation.
9) Prepares and coordinates print, out of home, and local cable insertion orders; maintains a chart of placements; joins Account Manager in magazine representative meetings.
10) Learns media billing process and executes billing.
11) Works with Traffic Department to traffic broadcast instructions and communicates with creative agency for traffic issues.
12) Develops and maintains positive relationships with media suppliers.
13) Develops opportunities to grow EM2 revenue within current clients.

### III. COMPETENCIES

#### *Communications*

Negotiating—dealing with others in order to reach an agreement or solution; for example, negotiating rates for magazine ads.

Persuading—dealing with others in order to influence them toward some action or point of view; for example, selling an idea to a peer or supervisor.

Interviewing—conducting interviews directed toward some specific objective; for example, interviewing experts during the problem-solving process.

Routine Information Exchange—giving or receiving job-related information.

Public Speaking—making formal presentation before internal audiences.

Writing—writing or dictating formal or informal communications, such as letters, reports, and e-mails.

Effective Listening—actively listens and engages in conversations in order to clearly understand others' message and intent

### Research

Using Public Records—conducts research using public records and documents, including library based and on-line resources.

Using Databases—develops database research skills such as knowledge and use of procedures, programs, and conventions for programs such as MRI and Scarborough.

Accessing Resources—identifies, locates, and utilizes targeted resources to fit research needs

### Entrepreneurism/Innovation

Unleashing Potential—creates systems such as information sharing to unleash individual and organizational potential.

Using Resources—understands how to use internal resources to generate new ideas and products.

Identifying Potential Barriers—identifies organizational barriers to innovation and recommends ways to remove existing or potential barriers.

### Customer Interface and Knowledge

Understanding of Clients—has a basic understanding of clients, their industry, and their products.

Meeting Client Needs—understands how to tap internal resources to meet client needs.

Client Interaction—periodically interacts with clients on a superficial level.

### Problem Solving

Analyzing Root Cause—using problem-solving techniques to identify problems on more than a superficial level.

Prioritizing—as a team member, weighing several solutions, such as promotion ideas, to identify and recommend the solution that will best solve the problem under discussion.

## Coaching/Mentoring

Providing Feedback—provides constructive criticism for team members regarding technical competencies and interpersonal relationships.

Identifying Resources—identifies need for professional development in the form of classes, books, Internet, etc. for professional development of self and coworkers

## Developing Goals and Objectives

Objective Setting—systematically assists in setting objectives and goals for self, the team and client needs, and develops tactics to achieve them.

Setting Priorities—assists in setting priorities based on the organization's mission and vision and organizes individual activities to address those priorities.

Establishing Measures—helps the team to establish quantifiable, specific success criteria for targeted objectives.

Articulating Objectives—clearly articulates objectives and goals to peers, customers, and managers.

Managing Resources—identifies and effectively uses resources such as people, technology, and time to achieve objectives.

## Project Management

Assisting—assisting with the achievement of tasks within a project by meeting assignment deadlines.

Coordinating—responsible for coordinating specific components of projects, such as approving buys.

Assigning—coordinating and assigning resources on a limited scale.

Profit Orientation—understands how EM2 makes a profit and their role in profitability.

Goal Setting—sets quantifiable, time-sensitive individual goals for project completion.

## Leadership

Modeling Behaviors—engages in professional behaviors and practices.

Creating a Healthy Work Environment—helps to develop a work climate conducive to productivity and employee motivation.

Managing Change—helps to develop processes that enable clients and peers to be adaptable to organizational change.

## Professional Integrity

Taking Ownership—taking responsibility for one's daily decisions and actions.

Seeking Clarification—proactively seeking clarification by asking questions about unclear tasks or responsibilities.

Clarifying Client Needs—proactively seeking clarification and understanding of clients' objectives from internal resources.

Resolving Conflicts—proactively attempting to resolve disagreements with coworkers, clients, and suppliers.

Compromising—seeking compromise in order to promote win–win interactions within the team.

Constructively Criticizing—providing constructive criticism in a positive manner.

Managing Emotions—handling feelings so that they are appropriate; finding ways to handle fears, anger, and anxiety professionally.

Empathizing—demonstrating sensitivity to others' feelings and concerns.

Contributing to Company Profitability—understanding and carrying out daily activities that positively impact organizational efficiency and effectiveness.

## IV. RELATIONSHIPS

1) Reports to Account Manager or Account Supervisor.
2) Establishes and maintains relationships with EM2 support teams.
3) Establishes and maintains relationships with clients assigned; works closely with the Account Manager to obtain required information for clients.
4) Attends meetings and maintains contact with media suppliers.
5) Attends meetings and maintains contact with creative agency staff.

## V. LEVEL: Exempt

## VI. EDUCATION AND EXPERIENCE REQUIRED

Bachelor's Degree and/or equivalent experience in a related field are required for this position.

## VII. TECHNOLOGY KNOW-HOW

This position requires a basic understanding of office software such as e-mail, MS Word, and Excel, as well as the ability to conduct basic Internet navigation activities.

# *Appendix 17*

## **Sample Career Matrix**

### Associate Account Manager—Account Manager—Account Supervisor

| Competency | Associate Level 1 | Associate Level 2 | Account Mgr Level 1 | Account Mgr Level 2 | Account Sup Level 1 | Account Sup Level 2 |
|---|---|---|---|---|---|---|
| Communications | Focus is on team and vendor interactions | Communications extended to periodic client interactions | Interactions include interviewing applicants and client presentations | Interactions with clients at higher frequency and level of sophistication | Communications include an advisory-counseling role for clients or Direct Reports | Client interactions have significant impact on company |
| Teamwork and Collaboration | Works collaboratively as member of account team | Works collaboratively with client contacts periodically | Role of facilitator and team leader becomes a focus | Selects methods for the team to accomplish objectives | Focus is on resource allocation And selecting and coaching team members | Focus shifts to developing company as a team to ensure organizational success |
| Research | Familiarity with accessing information using basic research tools | Occasionally must synthesize research and offer recommendations | Frequently analyzes the impact of research and projects potential scenarios | Periodically trains other staff on research methods | Maintains skills, but delegates and monitors research projects | Highest level of customer interface to explain research results |
| Competency | Associate Level 1 | Associate Level 2 | Account Mgr Level 1 | Account Mgr Level 2 | Account Sup Level 1 | Account Sup Level 2 |
| Entrepreneurism and Innovation | Takes initiative in generating ideas and finding creative solutions | Develops ways to remove existing or potential barriers | Models and promotes risk taking and leverages resources | Develops innovative products to recommend to clients | Envisions critical break-throughs to stay competitive becomes critical | Finds and allocates resources that support innovative practices |
| Customer Interface and Knowledge | Has a basic understanding of client's products; infrequent client contact | Frequently interacts with clients; increased understanding of customer's products | Has an in-depth understanding of clients and products; increased client contact | Frequent client interaction on substantive issues; increased understanding of client's industry | In-depth undertstanding of client's business practices; recommends solutions to meet future needs | Understands client's needs well enough to recommend enhancements to business processes |

| Problem Solving | Identifies core issues and proactively searches for options | Ability to select best approach toward problem solving | Objectively assesses and recommends potential solutions | Asssesses barriers to success and Implements solutions | May train client/ team members on problem solving methods | Approaches and defines problems from a company and client perspective |
|---|---|---|---|---|---|---|
| Competency | Associate Level 1 | Associate Level 2 | Account Mgr Level 1 | Account Mgr Level 2 | Account Sup Level 1 | Account Sup Level 2 |
| Coaching and Mentoring | Provides feedback and suggested resources for peers | a | Provides feedback and developmen-tal opportun-ities for Direct Reports | Assesses skills of team members and designs methods to enhance skills | Coaches and guides to ensure that skills of individual members and team collectively meet company objectives | Develops methods to recognize individual and team success |
| Setting Goals and Objectives | Sets objectives and goals that support team needs | Helps the team to set objectives and goals and develop measures | Identifies and uses team/ company resources to meet objectives | Assesses the support mechanisms and barriers in the client's industry and co. that affect goals | Synthesizes knowledge of client, client's industry, company, and other factors to implement strategic plans | Identifies critical checkpoints and evaluates success criteria against objectives; redirects resources if required |
| Project Management | Participates in segments of projects | Increased level of participation in range of projects | Supervises project segments and staff; designs timetables for completion | Sets project checkpoints; develops means to remove barriers | Balances project components to ensure least-best cost for best value | Shifts team priorities when required to meet client needs and ensure co. profitability |
| Competency | Associate Level 1 | Associate Level 2 | Account Mgr Level 1 | Account Mgr Level 2 | Account Sup Level 1 | Account Sup Level 2 |
| Leadership | Serves as a role model for peers in development of productive, customer oriented work behaviors and methods | Helps peers align their roles in relation to personal, department, and organizational objectives | Accepts ultimate accountability for work results of Direct Reports | Develops systems and procedures that produce customer oriented products and services | Identifies the need for changes required to meet the demands of constantly evolving customer requirements; recommends practices to address | Removes barriers to innovation within company and advises client contacts on internal processes to remain innovative |
| Professional Integrity | Takes ownership of daily decisions; team impact | Ownership impacts team, vendors | Ownership has impact on team, vendors, client contact at same level | Ownership has impact on team, vendors, clients, other Acct Mgrs | Ownership has impact on team, vendors, clients, co. colleagues | Ownership has impact on team, vendors, clients, company colleagues, and community |

## Appendix 18

### Self-Assessment on Emotional Intelligence

For each item, place the most accurate response to the left of each number.

| Rarely | Occasionally | Sometimes | Usually | Almost Always |
|:---:|:---:|:---:|:---:|:---:|
| **1** | **2** | **3** | **4** | **5** |

____1. I am careful about the implied meaning of words I use.

____2. I like scientific explanations.

____3. People seem to come to me when they need help solving quantitative problems.

____4. I see clear, precise pictures in my mind.

____5. I have the ability to decide which situations to get involved in that are good for me.

____6. I know why I believe what I believe.

____7. I am sensitive to the moods of others.

____8. I express myself easily in words or in writing.

____9. I enjoy reading all types of books.

____10. I use a logical, analytical process to solve problems.

____11. I don't get lost because I have a good sense of direction.

____12. I understand myself and consequently make good decisions about what to do in life.

____13. I'm persuasive when I try to influence others.

____14. My grammar is accurate most of the time.

____15. I don't accept others' information or stories at face value.

____16. I'm good at reading and following instructions.

____17. I find satisfaction in working with numbers.

____18. I can help others solve their problems.

____19. My inner self is my source of strength and renewal.

____20. I understand what motivates others, even when they try to hide their feelings.

____21. I like to experience what I'm learning about.

____22. I'm confident in my own opinions.

____23. I can interact in large groups.

____24. My feelings and emotions are my own responsibility.

____25. I have a large network of people that I turn to for their expertise and experience.

SCORING INSTRUCTIONS: Put the number value for each item you checked beside the item number. The area of Emotional Intelligence is at the top of each column.

| Verbal | Logic | Visual–Spatial | Intrapersonal | Interpersonal |
|--------|-------|----------------|---------------|---------------|
| Item #1 | Item #2 | Item #4 | Item #5 | Item #7 |
| Item #8 | Item #3 | Item #11 | Item #6 | Item #13 |
| Item #9 | Item #10 | Item #16 | Item #12 | Item #18 |
| Item #14 | Item #15 | Item #21 | Item #19 | Item #20 |
| | Item #17 | | Item #22 | Item #23 |
| | | | Item #24 | Item #25 |

TOTAL ___         TOTAL ___         TOTAL ___         TOTAL___         TOTAL___

## SCORING INTERPRETATION:

| | **Low** | **Moderate** | **High** |
|---|---------|--------------|----------|
| **Verbal:** | 4 to 8 | 9 to 16 | 17 to 20 |
| **Logic:** | 5 to 10 | 11 to 20 | 21 to 25 |
| **Visual–Spatial:** | 4 to 8 | 9 to 16 | 17 to 20 |
| **Intrapersonal:** | 6 to 12 | 13 to 24 | 25 to 30 |
| **Interpersonal:** | 6 to 12 | 13 to 24 | 25 to 30 |

| *SCORE* | *LEVEL OF COMPETENCY* |
|---------|------------------------|
| Low | You tend to avoid activities in this area, and it is not one of your strengths. Gaining competency in this area will take effort and patience. |
| Moderate | You tend to be comfortable with activities in this area, although you don't always go out of your way to use this competency. With some effort, you could achieve better results in this area and the experience would be very satisfying. |
| High | This is your comfort zone, where you show a high level of confidence and competency. You could become an expert in this area with little effort. |

# BIBLIOGRAPHY

Bar-On, R. (1997). *The Bar-On Emotional Quotient Inventory (EQ-i): A Test of Emotional Intelligence.* Toronto, Canada: Multi-Health Systems.

Bar-On, Reuven. (2000). *Baron Emotional Quotient Inventory.* Toronto, North Tonawanda: Multi-Health Systems.

Bar-On, R., and Handley, R. (2003b). *The Bar-On EQ-360: Technical Manual.* Toronto, Canada: Multi-Health Systems

Bar-on, R., and Parker, J. (2000). *The Handbook of Emotional Intelligence.* San Francisco: Jossey-Bass.

Becker, B., Huselid, M., and Ulrich, D. (2001). *The Hr Scorecard.* Boston: Harvard Business School Press.

Boyatzis, R. E., Cowan, S. S., and Kolb, D. A. (1995). *Innovations in Professional Education: Steps on a Journey to Learning.* San Francisco: Jossey-Bass.

Boyatzis and McKee. (2005). *Resonant Leadership,* Boston: Harvard Business School Press.

Bradberry, Travis and Greaves, Jean. (2005). *The Emotional Intelligence Quick Book: Everything You Need to Know to Put Your EQ to Work.* New York: Fireside.

Brookfield, S. (1996). "Breaking the Code: Engaging Practitioners in Critical Analysis of Adult Educational Literature." In R. Edwards, A. Hanson, and P. Raggatt (eds.), *Boundaries of Adult Learning* (57–81). London and New York: Routledge.

Brookfield, Steven D. (1995). *Becoming a Critically Reflective Teacher.* San Francisco: Josey-Bass.

Caruso, David R. and Salovey, Peter. (2004). *The Emotionallly Inelllighent Manager,* San Francisco: Jossey-Bass.

Cherniss, C., and Goleman, D. (2001). *The Emotionally Intelligent Workplace.* San Francisco: Jossey-Bass.

Cooper, Robert K., and Sawaf, Ayman. (1997). *Executive EQ: Emotional Intelligence in Leadership and Organizations.* New York: Grosset/Putnam.

Costa, P. T. Jr., and McCrae, R. R. (1997). "Longitudinal Stability of Adult Personality." In R. Hogan, J. A. Johnson, and S. R. Briggs (eds.), *Handbook of Personality Psychology* (269–290). New York: Academic Press.

Doll, Edgar A. "The Vineland Social Maturity Scale: Manual of Directions." *The Training School Bulletin,* 22 (1935): 1–3.

Drew, Todd. (2007). *"EI as a Predictor of Student Teacher Performance." University of Nebraska, Lincoln. Unpublished dissertation.*

George, J. "Emotions and Leadership: The Role of Emotional Intelligence." *Human Relations,* 53 (August 2000): 1027–1050.

Goleman, D. (1995). *Emotional Intelligence.* New York: Bantam Books.

———. (1998). *Working With Emotional Intelligence.* New York: Bantam.

Goleman, D., Boyatzis, and McKee. (2002). *Reawakening Your Passion for Work.* Cambridge, MA: Harvard Business Review.

Goleman, D., Boyatzis, R., and Mckee, A. (2002). *Primal Leadership.* Boston: Harvard Business School Press.

Holtz, Lou. (1998). *Winning Every Day.* New York: Harper Business.

Howard, Ann, and Wellins, Richard S. (2008). *The Global Leadership Forecast Study 2008/2009*. Pittsburgh, PA: Development Dimensions International.

Hughes, Marcia, Patterson, Bonita and Terrell, James Bradford. (2005). *Emotional Intelligence in Action*. San Francisco, CA: Pfeiffer.

Johnson and Blanchard (1998). *Who Moved My Cheese*. New York: G. P. Putnam Sons.

Lakein, Alan. (1996). *How to Get Control of Your Time and Your Life*. New York: New American Library.

Mayer, J. D., and Salovey, P. "The Intelligence of Emotional Intelligence," *Intelligence*, 17 (1993): 433–442.

———. (1997). "What Is Emotional Intelligence?" In P. Salovey and D. Sluyter (eds.), *Emotional Development and Emotional Intelligence: Implications for Educators* (3–34). New York: Basic Books.

Mayer, J. D., Salovey, P., and Caruso, D. R. (2002). *Mayer-Salovey-Caruso Emotional Intelligence Test (MSCEIT) Users Manual*. Toronto, Canada: MHS Publishers.

Morgan, G. (1988). *Riding the Waves of Change*. Jossey Bass, San Francisco, CA.

Orfalea, P., and Marsh, A. (2005). *Copy This!*. New York: Workman Pub.

Quenk, N. (1999). *Essentials of Myers-Briggs Type Indicator Assessment*. Hoboken, NJ: Wiley and Sons.

Richman, L. S. "How to Get Ahead in America." *Fortune*, May 16, 1994. 46–54, 18.

Salovey, P., and Mayer, J. D. "Emotional intelligence." *Imagination, Cognition, and Personality*, 9 (1990): 189.

Sternberg, R. (1996). *Successful Intelligence: How Practical and Creative Intelligence Determine Success in Life*. New York: Simon and Schuster.

Studer, Q. (2003). *Hardwiring Excellence*. Gulf Breeze: Fire Starter Pub.

Wechsler, D. (1981). *Wechsler Adult Intelligence Scale* (Rev. ed.). New York: Psychological Corporation.

Zeidner, M., Matthews, G. M., and Roberts, R. "Slow Down, You Move too Fast: Emotional Intelligence Remains an 'Elusive' Intelligence." *Emotion, 1 (2001)*: 265–275.

Zirkel, S. (2000). "Social Intelligence: The Development and Maintenance of Purposive Behavior." In R. Bar-On and J. D. A. Parker (eds.), *Handbook of Emotional Intelligence*. San Francisco: Jossey-Bass.

## Suggested Reading Lists

Albrecht, K., and Zemke, R. (2002). *Service America in the New Economy*. New York: McGraw-Hill.

Austin, J. (2000). *The Collaboration Challenge*. San Francisco: Jossey-Bass Publishers.

Beynon, D. "Your 'Emotional Intelligence?'" *Computerworld*, February 25, 2002

Buckingham, M., and Coffman, C. (1999). *First, Break All the Rules*. New York: Simon and Schuster.

Chrislip, D. (2002). *The Collaborative Leadership Fieldbook*. San Francisco: Jossey-Bass.

Cohen, A., and Bradford, D. (1990). *Influence Without Authority*. London: J. Wiley.

Daniel, D. "Soft Skills for CIOs and Aspiring CIOs: Four Ways to Boost Your Emotional Intelligence." *CIO Magazine*, June 25, 2007.

Fisher, R., Ury, W., and Patton, B. (1999). *Getting to Yes*. London: Random House Business Books.

Goleman, D. "What Makes a Leader." *Harvard Business Review*, January 2004.

Gostick, A., and Elton, C. (2007). *The Carrot Principle*. New York: Free Press.

Gravett, L., and Throckmorton, R. (2007). *Bridging the Generation Gap*. Franklin Lakes: Career Press.

Kaplan, R., and Norton, D. (1996). *The Balanced Scorecard*. Boston: Harvard Business School Press.

Karlin, D. "Are You Paying Attention to Your People." *Fast Company*, August, 2008.

Lynch, F. (2001). *The Diversity Machine*. New Brunswick: Transaction Publishers.

Morgan, G. (1988). *Riding the Waves of Change: Developing Managerial Competencies for a Turbulent World*. City: Jossey-Bass Inc Pub.

Murray, C. "Intelligence in the Classroom." *Wall Street Journal*, January 16, 2007.
Straus, D., and Layton, T. (2002). *How to Make Collaboration Work*. San Francisco: Berrett–Koehler Publishers.
Thomas, R. (1991). *Beyond Race and Gender*. New York: AMACOM, American Management Association.
Zwell, M., (2000). *Creating a Culture of Competence*. New York: Wiley.

## Web sites

### *EI Consortium*

The Consortium for Research on Emotional Intelligence in Organizations aids the advancement of research and practice related to emotional intelligence in organizations.
www.eiconsortium.org

# INDEX